ENJ

Or Cities Will Be No More is a message from God for this hour. Micah Wood was given this revelation from deep encounter and deep study. The journey you are about to take on the pages of this book will bring new understanding to old truths. Prepare yourself. The watchman in you is about to be awakened.

— KAREN WHEATON, THE RAMP

The need for watchmen in this hour is beyond urgent. The cities of the earth, including God's city, Jerusalem, must have intercessors and advocates taking their place "on the wall."

Micah Wood has heard, responded to, and is issuing this call with both prophetic unction and sound biblical teaching. I'm not sure if he's a prophet who teaches or a teacher who prophesies, but either way Micah delivers this message with clarity, precision, and force. Out of the whirlwind of this book, may God raise up today's Ezekiels, making us the watchmen He is looking for.

— ROBERT STEARNS, EAGLES' WINGS

We are living in the last "dayze." People are comfortably numb, and the watchman anointing has only fallen on a few. The heaviness of the eyelids of many ministers today is weighted with ease and comfort. But something is coming on the horizon, and we must have watchmen with a trumpeter's anointing! The Bible says CRY ALOUD, SPARE NOT . . . lift up your voice like a TRUMPET! We need voices that sound like a shofar in the enemy's camp! A WAKE-UP CALL! Micah Wood is one of those trumpets. This book will breathe life into your heart and mind with fresh wind to get back on that wall and sound an alarm. You are a VOICE for God and this book will awaken you! I fully endorse it, and I pray that you read it for the sake of our cities, nations, and world.

— MYLES RUTHERFORD, WORSHIP WITH WONDERS

I describe Micah Wood as a teaching priest who has been entrusted with deep insight from the Lord for our generation. His life of consecration and devotion in prayer makes him the right person to bring this powerful revelation on the call of the watchman to the body of Christ. I highly recommend this book to every believer.

— JAMES ALADIRAN, PRAYER STORM

OR CITIES WILL BE NO MORE
GOD IS LOOKING FOR WATCHMEN

MICAH WOOD

To my friend, Josh Hollingsworth, a true watchman

"And what I say to you, I say to all: Watch!"
Jesus, Mark 13:37

CONTENTS

PART ONE
INTRODUCTION

CHAPTER ONE

CAUGHT IN THE WHIRLWIND

"GOD IS LOOKING FOR WATCHMEN, OR CITIES WILL BE NO MORE." I wrote these words in my journal on June 14, 2020.

2020 had already been a turbulent year, and the chaos only continued to increase. In March, the Covid lockdowns began in America. "By April 2020, about half of the world's population was under some form of lockdown, with more than 3.9 billion people in more than 90 countries or territories having been asked or ordered to stay at home by their governments."[1] Then, in May, protests and riots began in the wake of George Floyd's death. American cities were quite literally burning. Floyd's death opened a volcanic fissure through which the ancient pain of racial injustice erupted. In November, the 2020 US presidential election exacerbated the year's difficulties as allegations of voter fraud fueled headlines. The election's prolonged controversy strained relationships in communities across the nation. The stability of American life seemed to teeter on a precipice. It felt like a dystopian novel.

And yet, as I wrote those words in the early morning hours of June 14, they were not a response to any of the situations I just described. The statement did not originate from my own assessment of the news cycles and current events. Those sobering words came to me through a God-encounter that reoriented my life.

Through a dream, God arrested my attention and gripped me with both a call and a message. This book is about that encounter and its aftermath.

The Watchman Dream

Dreams are funny things. Some you remember well after waking up. Others are bits of foggy images that invade your consciousness. Yet something may trigger your memory, helping you put together what it was you dreamed the night before. Then, there are those dreams you remember as soon as you wake up, and you sense they have some level of significance. They seem to contain God-language that you need to interpret and somehow apply to your life. And what about those dreams that are more than dreams? They are unforgettable God-encounters during the night. You do not simply remember them when you wake up. They jolt you awake into God-awareness, calling you to prayer! My watchman dream was one of those.

In the dream, I attended the First Wesleyan Church in Tuscaloosa, Alabama. It's not where I typically attended church, so I was there as a visitor. I sat in the sanctuary, wearing a blazer. The dress code in this church was more formal than the church I attended, so I was trying to dress appropriately. To my surprise, I started to feel a gentle breeze blowing, making me feel a bit chilly. The breeze was calm enough not to be disruptive, but strong enough for me to feel it despite the blazer. Logically, I figured the breeze should have come from an AC vent, yet I knew somehow it came from outside the church. That didn't make sense to my mind, though, because there was no outside access from the sanctuary. I turned to the gentleman beside me to say something about it, but I was interrupted. The wind suddenly became a whirlwind.

This whirlwind was forceful *and* disruptive, but it wasn't evil. I knew it was God. It picked up everyone in the sanctuary and carried us all around the room without any of us being harmed. We were flying together in the air, and I could feel the strength of this God-wind carrying me and swirling around me. I could also see the rest of the congregation in the air and instruments from the stage scattered about.

In a split second, a host of things ran through my mind. First, I was overwhelmed by the fact that I was experiencing God in a very tangible way. I knew this whirlwind was a God-manifestation, and I was physically feeling Him as wind on my skin. Within my heart, I had this sense of joyful refreshing mixed with awestruck wonder. I kept thinking, *God is real!* Before this moment, I knew God was real, but what I experienced then made me to know He *really* was real. I was laughing with tears on my cheeks at the mixture of holy emotions.

Secondly, I was shocked that this happened at a church where no one was asking for it or expecting it. They did not have an expectation for God to show up in that kind of way, and they certainly were not asking Him to. It made me rethink what God is capable of. He is not limited by our own expectation for Him. God can show up however and whenever He wants.

Thirdly, I was amazed that no one could stop this God-happening, though it was clearly disruptive to the order of service. Furthermore, this wind was not manufactured by man in any way. It was a wind from God that forcefully carried everyone with it. I thought to myself that this must have been what revivalists of old experienced—a wind that happened *to* them. It began to reshape my paradigm of revival as I realized that revival was something different than I had previously thought. Before this experience, I had associated revival with anointed preaching or prolonged church services—really good church due to charismatic ministers. This was not that. It was utterly God, and it was utterly refreshing. While in the air, I thought, *If this is revival, then I want to pray for revival again.*

Lastly, I knew that, when I would awake from this dream, I would have some homework to do. I needed to study the book of

Ezekiel because he encountered God in a similar way. I knew that I needed the reference point of Scripture to interpret rightly this experience and apply it faithfully to my own life.

The whirlwind then dropped me and a handful of men into the center of the sanctuary. I began to prophesy to them, not understanding what I said, but knowing it was from God. This was different than other times I had operated in spiritual gifts. Most of the time, the process went through inspiration, formulation, and articulation. In times past, I had received inspiration from the Holy Spirit. Then, I had formulated language around that idea to make it understandable to others. Finally, I had articulated it through speech. This prophecy bypassed that process. It didn't go through the progression of ear, mind, and mouth. It was as though God commandeered my mouth and used it without consulting my mind at all. I prophesied with an authority I had never known, saying, "God is looking for watchmen, or cities will be no more . . . like the nine cities in the west of Israel." As I said that, I thought to myself, *What cities? What am I talking about? Is this in the Bible? Is there some point in history where nine cities in Israel face judgment or destruction?*

I continued to prophesy and mentioned a significant name from Ezekiel (or connected to Ezekiel) that started with a "B." The name was significant because it would teach them about being watchmen. As I prophesied, I saw men and women in my mind's eye who were spiritually adopting cities to protect these cities through intercessory prayer. If they didn't act as watchmen for these cities, I knew the cities literally would become no more and would be forgotten.

As I finished speaking, my mind took control of my speech again. I looked at the group of men and asked rhetorically, "What does that even mean?" I laughed as I said it because, though the message I delivered was heavy, I was still refreshed and joyful from the wind of God. Besides, I was still a bit perplexed, not exactly knowing what the Spirit through me was referring to by "nine cities in the west of Israel." I continued to think to myself that I had some work to do, studying Ezekiel.

As the dream shifted toward the end, I thought two things: 1) *This dream is from God,* and 2) *God, don't let me forget this dream!*

Finally, as I started to leave First Wesleyan's sanctuary, I overheard the pastor or service emcee doing church announcements. I realized they had already put everything in the sanctuary back together and moved on with the service as if the whirlwind had never happened. It grieved me deeply because they experienced the whirlwind, but they didn't truly hear, receive, or apply the message that came out of the whirlwind. I knew they would tell the story of what happened but not embrace the God-ordained interruption to their lives.

The Dream's Aftermath

This dream jolted me awake in the early morning hours. I had the strong sense of God's presence in my bedroom, and I felt compelled to get up, write the dream down, and begin to process its message. As I did, God emphasized quite dramatically the component of cities as a focal point.

In the dream, I prophesied, "God is looking for watchmen, or cities will be no more . . . like the nine cities in the west of Israel." I began to do research, trying to find something that would give me clarity and interpretation about this statement. Specifically, I was looking for nine cities in the west of Israel that faced some kind of judgment or destruction.

Eventually, I came across a Bible commentary published in 1894 and written by James Glentworth Butler. The title of this volume is *Bible-Work: The Old Testament: Vol. 9: Ezekiel–Malachi.* As I read, I thought I was reading Butler's introduction to Ezekiel. Since the dream emphasized that book of the Bible, it made the most sense to start there. Butler described how the prophet in chapter 1, verses 10–15, "predicts the fate of the nine cities of the Shephelah."[2] When I read "nine cities," I was stunned that there was an actual biblical reference that corresponded to my dream. Furthermore, the word *Shephelah* referred to a region of lowlands in Israel that was *west* of Jerusalem, between the mountains and the coastal plains.[3] Amazed yet excited about what I found, I couldn't wait to read this passage for myself in Scripture.

I then turned to Ezekiel 1:10–15. When I got there, I ran into a problem. Those verses mentioned nothing about the nine cities. In fact, those verses didn't mention even one city. Confused, I turned back to the Butler commentary. I had assumed that I was reading an introduction to Ezekiel. As I flipped to the beginning of the chapter in the commentary, I was shocked to discover that I was actually reading an introduction to the prophet Micah. As I read my very own name on the page, a sober sense of God's reality overwhelmed my heart. It confirmed to me that this was no mere dream that I could simply discard or ignore. This was a word from God for my life, and I had to receive it, live it, and share it with others.

I then turned to Micah 1:10–15, and I read clearly about the nine cities in Israel that Micah named: Shaphir, Zaanan, Beth Ezel, Maroth, Lachish, Moresheth Gath, Achzib, Mareshah, and Adullam.* I grabbed another commentary to read further about this passage, and it confirmed their location in the land: "Places named in [verses] 10–15 were in *west* Judah, in Micah's home territory. They were devastated by the Assyrians, along with the overthrow of the Northern Kingdom."[4] *Nine cities in the west of Israel had been devastated by judgment.*

God's emphasis upon cities throughout the dream didn't stop there. I had this dream on a Sunday, and later that day I led a prayer meeting at church. I was so excited about the dream that I shared it with the prayer team. One of the leaders present was my

---

* Micah also addressed Gath and Beth Aphrah, but they were cities of the Philistines.

friend, Josh Hollingsworth. As I told the dream, the Holy Spirit brought a woman's name to Josh's mind. It was Linda. She coordinates a national intercessory prayer network that Josh has led via conference call from time to time. Josh knew that he needed to share my dream with her because it would encourage the prayer network about being watchmen for cities. Josh was unable to contact her in that moment, though, because he had left his phone at home.

After the church service that night, Josh found his phone and was surprised to see that Linda had already texted him about five times. She was urgently trying to contact him to see if he was available to lead that week's prayer call. What's more, she first had started texting him at the same time he thought about her name during the prayer meeting! Josh knew all of this was confirmation that the prayer network needed to hear the dream.

A couple days later, Josh led the prayer call and told them the dream. When he was done sharing it, Linda was astonished. She said on the phone to the network, "Guys, I didn't tell him! I didn't tell him!"

Intrigued, Josh asked, "You didn't tell me what?"

Linda explained that, that morning, the entire prayer network was finishing a nine-day fast in which they were praying for nine cities in America. *Their goal in the nine-day fast was to serve as watchmen for each of the nine cities.* When Josh recounted this story to me, I was left speechless and amazed. What were the chances that this intercessory group would target *nine cities* and would take their place as watchmen? The level of emphasis and confirmation that God gave me regarding this dream revealed the level of urgency within His heart. And the message became very clear to me at that point. I knew for a fact that *God is looking for watchmen because God loves cities, and without the watchmen, cities will be no more.*

What's at Stake?

If we ignore the message of the dream and, subsequently, this book, cities are at stake. While I hope this book is inspirational and educational, its ultimate purpose is missional. It doesn't simply aim to enrich your devotional life. It is anchored in the gravity of missional necessity. God cares about cities because God cares about people. When the prophet Jonah didn't have pity on Nineveh, God rebuked him. He described His own compassion for the city, asking, "And should not I pity Nineveh, that great city, in which there are more than 120,000 persons. . . ?" (4:11). Because of His love for people, God sent Jonah on an errand of mercy to a city. The buildings weren't what caught God's attention. It was the inhabitants who were lost in spiritual darkness, those who could not "discern between their right hand and their left hand" (Jon. 4:11 KJV). *The God who loved cities then is the God who is looking for watchmen now.*

CHAPTER TWO

CITIES WILL BE NO MORE

Before we look closer at the vocation of watchmen, let's consider the statement, "Cities will be no more." That's a strong statement with an intense message. It's frightening, even. Why will cities be no more? What will be the source of their destruction?

One of the complexities of God is that He is simultaneously Advocate and Judge. On one hand, from His heart flows tender mercy that cries out compassionately for our broken condition. On the other hand, from His mouth issues righteous judgment that holds us accountable for our rebellion, assessing and revealing the decisions we have made that have created our condition. At times, it's difficult for our minds to reconcile this dual reality. How can God act in both ways, both defending us and judging us? Is this not a conflict of interest?

When we find ourselves perplexed by the nature of God, A.W. Tozer offers words of insight in his book *The Knowledge of the Holy*:

> If all this appears self-contradictory—*Amen*, be it so. The various elements of truth stand in perpetual antithesis, sometimes requiring us to believe apparent opposites while we wait for the moment when we shall know as we are known. Then truth which

> now appears to be in conflict with itself will arise in shining unity
> and it will be seen that the conflict has not been in the truth but in
> our sin-damaged minds.[1]

From Scripture, we must hold the tension of truth, which requires us "to believe apparent opposites." God is Advocate, and God is Judge. God forgives us, and God holds us accountable. God is looking for watchmen so that cities will be spared, and God will condemn cities based upon their actions.

It may be odd for our modern minds to conceive of God acting toward cities in wrath, leading to their destruction. However, Scripture gives us plenty of reference points to furnish our imaginations. Most people are familiar with the Tower of Babel in Genesis 11, for example. We often overlook, though, that it wasn't just a tower that men built. *It was a city.* Genesis 11:4, says, "And they said, 'Come, let us build ourselves *a city*, and a tower whose top is in the heavens.'" When God assessed the situation, He didn't just review the tower. He reviewed the city: "But the LORD came down to see the city and the tower which the sons of men had built" (Gen. 11:5). Next, He acted according to His assessment: "So the LORD scattered them abroad from there over the face of all the earth, and they ceased building the city" (Gen. 11:8). *God's judgment caused the city to be no more.* Why God chose to do this is a bit of a different topic. My point right now is that God's judgment—His assessment and corresponding actions—directly determined the destiny of the city.

Another example is the case of Sodom and Gomorrah in Genesis 18 and 19. Like Babel, the story begins with God's descent to take assessment. Genesis 18:20–21 explains, "And the LORD said, 'Because the outcry against Sodom and Gomorrah is great, and because their sin is very grave, I will go down now and see whether they have done altogether according to the outcry against it that has come to Me; and if not, I will know.'" God was interested in the condition of the two cities, and He personally investigated the things He had heard about them. Based upon what He found, He acted accordingly. Though the sexual sin of Sodom is typically what most people think about first, God explained in Ezekiel 16:49–50 that its sin was much more multifaceted than just that: "Look, this was the iniquity of your sister Sodom: She and her daughter had pride, fullness of food, and abundance of idleness; neither did she strengthen the hand of the poor and needy. And they were haughty and committed abomination before Me; therefore I took them away as I saw fit." The injustices of the city provoked an outcry, which reached God's ears. After He investigated, He decided He must destroy the city. The men (or angels) God sent to Sodom on His behalf explained to Lot, "Have you anyone else here? . . . whomever you have in the city—take them out of this place! For we will destroy this place, because the outcry against them has grown great before the face of the LORD, and the LORD has sent us to destroy it" (Gen. 19:12–13). After God's dealing with Sodom and Gomorrah, they become no more: "So He [the LORD] overthrew those cities, all the plain, all the inhabitants of the cities, and what grew on the ground" (Gen. 19:25).

After reading about these three cities—Babel, Sodom, and Gomorrah—we may think to ourselves, *Well, that was the God of the Old Testament. He doesn't act that way anymore. He doesn't kill people in judgment, and He certainly doesn't judge or destroy cities.* It's common to respond in that way to Old Testament accounts of God's wrath. However, a quick glance at the New Testament may cause us to rethink our easy dismissal of His judgments and His wrath.

Judgment in the New Testament

The book of Acts occurs after the death, burial, resurrection, and ascension of Jesus. I point this out because *many people's atonement theology leaves no room for God to display wrath toward humans after the gospel events of Jesus's life.* In two specific accounts, however, people died in ways directly connected to God's judgment. In Acts 5:1–11, a husband and wife, Ananias and Sapphira, lied to God. Immediately, they dropped dead in front of the apostles. The early church had a real-time example of Paul's words in Ephesians 5:6: "Let no one deceive you with empty words, for because of these things the wrath of God comes upon the sons of disobedience." It's interesting that Paul began this statement about wrath with "let no one deceive you." Paul seemed to anticipate the day when "empty words" would try to erase the reality of God's judgment. Tozer weighed in on this as well:

> But God's justice stands forever against the sinner in utter severity. The vague and tenuous hope that God is too kind to punish the ungodly has become a deadly opiate for the consciences of millions. It hushes their fears and allows them to practice all pleasant forms of iniquity while death draws every day nearer and the command to repent goes unregarded. As responsible moral beings we dare not so trifle with our eternal future.[2]

In harmony with Paul, Tozer looked directly at God's judgment and recognized its reality. Though our flesh may want to mute or deny it, "as responsible moral beings," we must fully acknowledge it.

In Acts 12, we read about another death, that of Herod. The people of Tyre and Sidon flattered him with words of praise, saying, "The voice of a god and not of a man!" (Acts 12:22). The next verse explained the result: "Then immediately an angel of the Lord struck him, because he did not give glory to God. And he was eaten by worms and died" (Acts 12:23). It's hard to imagine that this "angel of the Lord" acted independently from God's instruction. Psalm 103:20 tells us that "His angels . . . do His word, heeding the voice of His word." Thus, Herod's death was not merely coincidental. Nor was he the victim of a rogue, zealous angel. Instead, God judged him according to his actions. In these two instances, we find continuity between God's wrath in the Old Testament and His wrath in the New Testament.

This principle of judgment, active in the pages of the New Testament, should have a profound impact upon the way we think about cities and God's assessment of them. Jesus Himself called our attention to the judgment of God regarding cities. Consider this passage from Matthew 11:20–24:

> Then He began to rebuke the cities in which most of His mighty works had been done, because they did not repent: "Woe to you, Chorazin! Woe to you, Bethsaida! For if the mighty works which were done in you had been done in Tyre and Sidon, they would have repented long ago in sackcloth and ashes. But I say to you, it will be more tolerable for Tyre and Sidon in the day of judgment than for you. And you, Capernaum, who are exalted to heaven, will be brought down to Hades; for if the mighty works which were done in you had been done in Sodom, it would have remained until this day. But I say to you that it shall be more tolerable for the land of Sodom in the day of judgment than for you."

In this passage, Jesus lamented the lack of repentance in three cities: Chorazin, Bethsaida, and Capernaum. During His ministry, Jesus performed "most of His mighty works" in them. He especially favored Capernaum, not just visiting the city, but dwelling within it (see Matt. 4:13). (Perhaps, this is why He described it as being "exalted to heaven.") His works within the cities, though, did not satisfy His heart. He wasn't merely interested in performing miracles there. He wanted the miracles to change the heart condition of the people. He wanted the signs to reorient their affections around Him, leading to deep transformation of their actions. When they failed to respond to Him through repentance, He didn't see it as merely a missed opportunity. He referred to something larger coming. He referred to the "day of judgment" and what each of these cities will face on that day. Each of them will be held accountable by God for what they did and did not do.

Not surprisingly, Jesus used Sodom as a reference point when talking about this reality. It was a city God assessed and God judged. *In using Sodom, Jesus was taking it out of the category of ancient, irrelevant history and putting it into the category of contemporary, relevant reality.* He wanted Chorazin, Bethsaida, and Capernaum to consider Sodom and learn from its destruction. Then, in Matthew 10, Jesus expanded Sodom's lesson beyond these three cities and applied it to all cities. As He sent out His disciples, He said to them, "And whoever will not receive you nor hear your words, when you depart from that house or city, shake off the dust from your feet. Assuredly, I say to you, it will be more tolerable for the land of Sodom and Gomorrah in the day of judgment than for that city!" (Matt. 10:14–15). He again used Sodom as a reference point to warn cities about the "day of judgment." If the cities didn't receive His disciples, they wouldn't simply miss an opportunity. God would hold them accountable for their lack of repentance.

Deferred Judgment: The Day of the Lord

Let's consider further the day of judgment and how it shapes the way we understand the world today and the trajectory of the future. Presently, it can seem as though God no longer holds man accountable for his actions. It can seem as though the God who acted in judgment in the Bible has disappeared from today's world. There is so much evil that occurs, seemingly unchecked and undeterred. As we read headlines and watch the news, we can identify with the words of Jeremiah 12:1: "Righteous are You, O LORD, when I plead with You; yet let me talk with You about Your judgments. Why does the way of the wicked prosper? Why are those happy who deal so treacherously?" Jeremiah saw an apparent gap between what the wicked *should* experience and what the wicked *actually* experience.

According to God's character, He should hold the wicked accountable for their deeds, yet Jeremiah saw their prosperity instead. How do we reconcile this?

Psalm 37 thoroughly addresses the dilemma, saying, "Do not fret because of evildoers, nor be envious of the workers of iniquity. For they shall soon be cut down like the grass, and wither as the green herb. . . . The wicked plots against the just, and gnashes at him with his teeth. The Lord laughs at him, for He sees that *his day is coming*" (1–2, 12–13). God will indeed judge evildoers, but He is deferring the full day of accountability to the future. That future date is the day of judgment, also described throughout the prophets as the "day of the Lord." It's not that God no longer holds man accountable for his rebellion. It's that the fullness of His assessment and fit response will happen at a future time. This is what Paul described in Romans 2 as he addressed impenitent man:

> But in accordance with your hardness and your impenitent heart you are treasuring up for yourself wrath in the day of wrath and revelation of the righteous judgment of God, who "will render to each one according to his deeds" . . . in the day when God will judge the secrets of men by Jesus Christ, according to my gospel. (Romans 2:5–6, 16)

Disobedience seems to go unnoticed by God right now. However, Paul claimed the full rendering of our actions does not happen right now. That will come in "the day of . . . revelation of the righteous judgment of God." *God defers the wrath man deserves today until the "day of wrath," which, for now, is not today.*

Why God does this is fully known only to Himself. However, Scripture does give us some glimpses into the reason. It is because "the Judge of all the earth" has a propensity toward compassionate mercy (Gen. 18:25). As He defers the full consequence of our actions, it gives us time to repent of our actions, seek Him for mercy, and amend our ways.

In one of his Epistles, Peter described this combination of future judgment, deferred wrath, and present mercy:

> But the heavens and the earth which are now preserved by the same word, are reserved for fire until the day of judgment and perdition of ungodly men. But, beloved, do not forget this one thing, that with the Lord one day is as a thousand years, and a thousand years as one day. The Lord is not slack concerning His promise, as some count slackness, but is longsuffering toward us, not willing that any should perish but that all should come to repentance. (2 Peter 3:7–9)

With certainty and conviction, Peter affirmed "the day of judgment and perdition of ungodly men." Why hasn't that day come yet? He explained that God is "longsuffering." This compassionate God doesn't want any to "perish." Thus, He is extending time "that all should come to repentance." *Deferred judgment gives man time to prepare for judgment.*

Here is a helpful, though very inadequate, example. When I graduated from university, I had accumulated thousands of dollars of debt. I had taken out student loans to pay for my education and living expenses. Upon graduating, the financial institutions gave me an option either to begin payments immediately or to defer payments to a future date. They understood that, as a recent graduate, I needed time to secure both a job and an income. They knew I would be unprepared if the full reckoning of my debt began immediately. The deferment did not cancel my debt. I still owed them thousands of dollars. However, it gave me time to adequately prepare myself to repay the debt.

In a similar yet far greater way, God knows that we cannot bear the full reckoning of our actions right now. Furthermore, He is giving us the opportunity to change our actions because He does not take pleasure in the destruction of man. He makes this abundantly clear in passages like Ezekiel 33. Within it, He reveals His passion for man's wellbeing and His strategy for man's transformation. That strategy includes revealing future judgment so that man may repent of his deeds before the day of judgment comes. In Ezekiel 33:14–16, God said, "Again, when I say to the wicked, 'You shall surely die,' if he turns from his sin and does what is lawful and right, . . . he shall surely live; he shall not die. None of his sins which he has committed shall be remembered against him; he has done what is lawful and right; he shall surely live." God warns the wicked about the ultimate end of their decisions to give them a jolt of reality. In doing so, the jolt hopefully invokes personal assessment that leads to change. *God does not reveal looming judgment because the condition of man is a foregone conclusion. He speaks about judgment because He is merciful.* If we don't realize that mercy motivates His revelation of judgment, then we'll misinterpret that revelation as God's desire toward us. We will think God takes pleasure in wrath. This misunderstanding of God is something He deals with in Ezekiel 33:10–11:

> Therefore you, O son of man, say to the house of Israel: "Thus you say, 'If our transgressions and our sins lie upon us, and we pine away in them, how can we live?'" Say to them: "As I live," says the Lord GOD, "I have no pleasure in the death of the wicked, but that the wicked turn from his way and live. Turn, turn from your evil ways! For why should you die, O house of Israel?"

God knew that as Ezekiel confronted Israel for her sin and described the ensuing consequences, Israel was likely to respond with hopelessness, claiming "we pine away," wondering "how can we live?" God emphatically dismantled that hopelessness, stating clearly He had "no pleasure" in their destruction. Instead, He was pleased with the repentance of the wicked, seeing them "turn from [their] way and live." Then, He called out passionately to Israel, "Turn, turn!" He repeated the call because of the intensity of His desire for her to obey it. He didn't utter a casual, one-time, "Turn," and then leave Israel to accept it or reject it. He drove the matter into her heart and then asked, "Why should you die?" It was not His desire for Israel to die, and it was not her predetermined end. *The revelation of future judgment and the time in-between gave Israel an opportunity to change.*

If we understand that God's mercy motivates Him to speak about judgment, then we are much more likely to listen when He speaks about judgment. Too often, we don't have space to hear something like, "cities will be no more," because we think a revelation of judgment contradicts God's attribute of mercy. We grow deaf, then, to His warnings because we do not think God would speak or act in those ways. However, *His mercy both reveals and defers judgment that we may repent.*

When Scripture recounts the fall of Jerusalem in 2 Chronicles 36, it includes God's prelude to that event:

> And the LORD God of their fathers sent warnings to them by His messengers, rising up early and sending them, because He had compassion on His people and on His dwelling place. But they mocked the messengers of God, despised His words, and scoffed at His prophets, until the wrath of the LORD arose against His people, till there was no remedy. (2 Chronicles 36:15–16)

Why did God send warnings? It was "because He had compassion." Had the people of Israel listened, the warnings could have been a prelude to repentance and life rather than a prelude to wrath and death.

Revelation 2 records a similar message. In His letter to the church in Thyatira, Jesus identified a problem. The people tolerated Jezebel, and it led to sexual immorality among God's servants. We may wonder, *Since this woman was not only living sinfully, but also influencing others to do the same, why hadn't Jesus dealt with her yet?* He explained, "I gave her time to repent of her sexual immorality, and she did not repent" (Rev. 2:21). He deferred judgment to give her an opportunity for repentance. Her time of reckoning had come. However, there was still a time for those who had joined her to turn. Jesus said, "Indeed I will cast her into a sickbed, and those who commit adultery with her into great tribulation, *unless they repent of their deeds*" (Rev. 2:22). If they would repent, they would not have to experience "great tribulation." Jesus would spare them the difficulty if they turned to Him.

Let's now apply what we've learned to the theme of cities. According to Matthew 11:20–24, future judgment is not just for individuals. God will also assess cities, and He will determine their future based upon what He finds. When this happened to Babel, Sodom, and Gomorrah, they became no more. Considering them as reference points, we ought to think soberly about the cities of the earth. We need to look at them in light of their spiritual condition. Financial prosperity can be deceiving. In Revelation, Babylon is a luxurious city, but its destruction comes in "one day" and "in one hour" (Rev. 18:8, 10). Our assessment of cities will be wrong if we merely use material metrics. We need to find the spiritual pulse.

As we think soberly, we ought to think hopefully as well. Today is another day of mercy and deferred judgment. *If wrath has not come, it's because wrath can still be avoided.* God's propensity and desire are for life—not death. Furthermore, God has revealed how we can alter the course of cities. Since He doesn't want them to be "no more," He is looking for watchmen.

PART TWO
THE CHARACTERISTICS
OF THE WATCHMEN

CHAPTER THREE

HOLY INTERRUPTION

If watchmen are God's answer to the dilemma of cities, it is incumbent upon us to understand who and what they are. We need to avoid the mistake of the church in my dream. The people at that church heard the message, but they didn't receive and apply it. We must hear, receive, learn, and apply what we learn with a sense of missional gravity and compassionate urgency. *Cities are dying for, and God is looking for, watchmen.*

To understand the call and vocation of the watchman, studying the book of Ezekiel is essential. Through a dramatic encounter, God made Ezekiel a watchman for the house of Israel. This happened in the whirlwind.

At the opening of the book of Ezekiel, Ezekiel described how he "saw visions of God" and "the word of the Lord came expressly" to him (1:1, 3). It's important to consider the way in which God revealed Himself to Ezekiel because it's an indicator of Ezekiel's assignment and his message. Though each revelation of God in Scripture fits together in perfect unity and harmony, God didn't always reveal Himself in the same way. *The way He reveals Himself to someone identifies the way He wants to reveal Himself through that person to others.* Thus, it's not just a personal revelation, but an indicator of the individual's assignment. Since the book of Ezekiel instructs us in the call and vocation of the watchman as well as serves as the backdrop for understanding my dream and its application, we need to consider the specific revelation Ezekiel saw about God and how it shaped his life's message.

When Ezekiel saw "visions of God," the whirlwind took centerstage as one of the most prominent and repetitive features. After his brief introduction, Ezekiel recorded, "Then I looked, and behold, a whirlwind was coming out of the north, a great cloud with raging fire engulfing itself; and brightness was all around it and radiating out of its midst like the color amber, out of the midst of the fire" (1:4). This fiery whirlwind descended upon him in chapter one, but it didn't stop there as it showed up to Ezekiel throughout the book. Later, in chapter three, he wrote, "So I arose and went out into the plain, and behold, the glory of the LORD stood there, like the glory which I saw by the River Chebar; and I fell on my face" (3:23). The glory he saw was the fiery whirlwind. This time, though, the whirlwind was showing up in "the plain" (3:22–23). In chapter eight, Ezekiel didn't just *see* the whirlwind, but the hand of the Lord brought Ezekiel *into* the whirlwind: "He stretched out the form of a hand, and took me by a lock of my hair; and the Spirit lifted me up between earth and heaven, and brought me in visions of God to Jerusalem. . . . And behold, the glory of the God of Israel was there, like the vision that I saw in the plain" (8:3–4). The prophet continued to reference former encounters with the whirlwind to describe the fresh encounters. Apparently, this was the way God wanted to reveal Himself to Ezekiel.

Why was the whirlwind such a feature within Ezekiel's "visions of God"? It introduces us to the first characteristic of the watchman: holy interruption. The call of the watchman is an *interruption*—not an addition. God intended for Ezekiel's experience with Him to be interruptive in nature. What God called Ezekiel to do reoriented Ezekiel's entire world. It didn't simply add a new facet of seeing God. This became all-consuming for the prophet.

You see, a whirlwind does not adjust itself to your convenience. You must adjust to its violent force. I'm from the state of Alabama. We are quite familiar with tornadoes. They are very, very disruptive. When a tornado siren sounds, you simply stop whatever you are doing and act in response to the tornado's threat. There is no negotiation or compromise with a tornado. Wherever it goes, the atmosphere changes, and everything revolves around it. This was God's point in His dealing with Ezekiel.

God did not reveal visions of Himself to Ezekiel merely to increase Ezekiel's knowledge. God didn't just drop by to have a casual conversation and let Ezekiel keep living his life per what was usual for him. *God showed up as a whirlwind because He was disrupting and interrupting Ezekiel's life. He was rearranging Ezekiel's priorities and drawing the prophet into His own priorities.* God brought Ezekiel into the world that revolved around Himself, the burning Man at the center of it all. By the end of the first encounter, you can see the effect: "Then I came to the captives at Tel Abib, who dwelt by the River Chebar; and I sat where they sat, and remained there astonished among them seven days" (3:15). The whirlwind encounter left Ezekiel overwhelmed, astonished, and speechless for seven days. It rocked his world.

What motivated this holy interruption from God? What was so urgent that God must manifest Himself to Ezekiel in this extraordinary way?

Amber Heart

Ezekiel recorded a detail of the whirlwind that is easy to overlook, but it holds an important insight: "Brightness was all around it and radiating out of its midst like the color of amber, out of the midst of the fire" (1:4). From within the whirlwind, the color amber radiated with brightness that illuminated the entire atmosphere. Though the entire whirlwind was a "raging fire," it seemed this radiant amber was a distinct part of the whirlwind that came from within it and was not a result of the flames. What caused this amber radiance, and what made it so prominent that its color overtook even the glow of the fire?

There are two other places in Ezekiel where the prophet mentioned the color amber. Both described it as originating from the same place:

> And above the firmament over their heads was the likeness of a throne, in appearance like a sapphire stone; on the likeness of the throne was a likeness with the appearance of a man high above it. Also from the appearance of His waist and upward I saw, as it were, the color of amber with the appearance of fire all around within it; and from the appearance of His waist and downward I saw, as it were, the appearance of fire with brightness all around. (Ezekiel 1:26–27)

> Then I looked, and there was a likeness, like the appearance of fire —from the appearance of His waist and downward, fire; and from His waist and upward, like the appearance of brightness, like the color of amber. (Ezekiel 8:2)

Ezekiel saw the throne of God. As he saw it, he used the language of earthly colors and objects to describe what he saw. As Ezekiel saw "a likeness with the appearance of a man high above" the throne, he made a distinction between "His" body above the waist and below the waist. Above the waist was on fire. Below the waist was on fire. Why, though, did Ezekiel distinguish between the two? Why not just say that His whole body was a fire? There was one difference between the two halves of the body and the quality of the fire. From the Man's waist upward, Ezekiel saw "the color of amber with the appearance of fire all around within it." Amber was present within the Man's upper body and not His lower body. Why? Perhaps, it was because the heart of God is the color amber, beating within His chest. Perhaps, it was this amber-hued heart that radiated brighter than fire, giving meaning, shape, and understanding to everything else Ezekiel experienced. Perhaps, Ezekiel knew that this amber heart was at the center of it all, and he wanted to make sure we did not miss it amid all the other sensational details of his encounter.

If you consider John's encounter with God in the book of Revelation, the amber hue showed up there, too, though John described it slightly differently: "Immediately, I was in the Spirit; and behold, a throne set in heaven, and One sat on the throne. And He who sat there was like a jasper and a sardius stone in appearance" (Rev. 4:2–3). The combination of jasper and sardius is very similar to amber. Ezekiel's and John's visions are comparable, seeing the throne of God and One upon the throne. From the throne of God, an amber heart beats, illuminating the atmosphere with a rich depth of holy passion.

If you consider the color amber, it's not a one-dimensional color. It has movement and a mixture of hues. It draws you into its depths and surrounds you with the sensation of warmth. It's no wonder this color radiates from the chest of God. How complex, deep, warm, and passionate the heart of God must be!

Now, let's bring this idea back to Ezekiel's original description of the whirlwind. Amber not only radiated from the upper half of the burning Man, but it was found radiating from the center of the whirlwind. Why? *Perhaps, the whirlwind was an external expression of God's internal reality. Perhaps, the whirlwind came to interrupt Ezekiel's world to reorient him around the passion of God's heart and agenda.* God's love for Israel couldn't stay quiet, silent, and calm. It swept Ezekiel into its force and fury, transforming him into a vessel that could fitly carry God's message.

When you consider other details in Ezekiel's encounter, it's not farfetched to think that an internal reality of God's Spirit was expressed externally through a distinct manifestation. Ezekiel described this paradigm in other ways. One of the most memorable features of Ezekiel was his description of the living creatures and how each of them were accompanied by "a wheel in the middle of a wheel" (1:16). As the living creatures moved, the wheels moved. Ezekiel explained why, writing, "Wherever the spirit wanted to go, they went, because there the spirit went . . . for the spirit of the living creatures was in the wheels" (1:20). The wheels were not merely mechanisms that assisted the living creatures. The wheels contained the *spirit* of the living creatures. They were a visible expression of the creatures' spiritual characteristics. If you'd like to know what the creatures' internal world was like, look at the wheels. In the same way, the fiery whirlwind was not just a mechanism God used to arrest Ezekiel. It was a visible, tangible experience Ezekiel had with God's internal world. The amber heart within the Man's chest became an amber whirlwind outside of His chest, interrupting Ezekiel and introducing him to His agenda.

When God interrupts us, it's not because He enjoys our inconvenience. He interrupts us because we've grown numb to the passion of His heart. We've grown unaware of the depth of His love. From His amber heart, a whirlwind issues with a force and fury that we can't ignore. It draws us back into orbit around His heart.

Disruption to and through Ezekiel

God dealt with Ezekiel in this way because He wanted to disrupt Ezekiel's world and because He wanted to do the same thing *through* Ezekiel. Throughout the book, God instructed Ezekiel to do odd, shocking things and to prophesy difficult, yet hopeful, prophecies. *The point was to use the prophet as a whirlwind to others.* The point was to use his voice to disrupt people's daily lives and call them to realign with God. Ezekiel disrupted others' priorities and called his hearers back into a world that revolved around God.

If you remember, my dream ended on a bit of a tragic note.

After the whirlwind left the sanctuary, everything went back to normal. I'm grieved because I know the church missed the point of the encounter. God didn't manifest Himself in that way only to give them an unusual experience or a sensational story. *God manifested in the whirlwind to interrupt their plans and call them to Himself.* Sadly, we human beings tend to overlook the purpose behind an encounter with God and simply settle for the encounter. We must see the purpose behind the encounter is to commission us with God's agenda.

I'm beginning with the whirlwind feature because it's important to know from the outset of this book what God has in mind. He doesn't simply want to add another biblical topic to your repertoire of understanding. That's not the point of the dream or this book. God wants to interrupt you. He wants to commission you with a fresh call, a disruptive call. *The whirlwind doesn't only come to refresh you, though it will. The whirlwind comes to rearrange you.*

CHAPTER FOUR

FRIENDSHIP WITH GOD

FOR WHAT PURPOSE DID EZEKIEL'S WHIRLWIND AND MY WHIRLWIND show up? Why the disruption? Once the whirlwind dropped me to the ground, I said these words in the dream: "God is looking for watchmen." Clearly, the whirlwind's purpose was to commission me with a new priority: the priority of being a watchman. The call to be a watchman was also the result of Ezekiel's encounter with the whirlwind. God interrupted him to commission him with this assignment. God's whirlwind dropped Ezekiel by the River Chebar in Ezekiel 3:15, leaving the prophet astonished. *The call to be a watchman was so significant that God used an extreme measure to arrest Ezekiel's attention, ensuring he wouldn't ignore or neglect the call.* As Ezekiel sat, pondering the encounter, God spoke to him, giving an explanation of its purpose: "Now it came to pass at the end of seven days that the word of the LORD came to me, saying, 'Son of man, I have made you a watchman for the house of Israel'" (3:16–17).

What does it look like to be a watchman? If this is who God's looking for and if the destinies of cities depend upon watchmen, it's important to define who they are and what their role is. Let's begin with a working description of the watchmen, and then we'll spend the rest of the book sketching out different features of their lives and actions.

In the context of friendship with God, watchmen cultivate prophetic sensitivity, intercessory love, and missional obedience for the sake of cities and nations.

———

Friendship with God is the foundation of being a watchman. If that isn't the starting point and the context, then watchmen will not fulfill their call faithfully with longevity. In Genesis 18, Abraham took the role of a watchman for the city of Sodom. Though the city was ultimately destroyed, the intercession of Abraham gave it an opportunity to be spared. The whole episode began when God shared with Abraham His secret counsel regarding the city. Genesis 18:17 records, "And the LORD said, 'Shall I hide from Abraham what I am doing . . . ?'" Commenting on this scripture, Lou Engle asks, "Who do you share your secrets with? Your friends."[1] You see, Scripture doesn't just refer to Abraham as a patriarch or a man of faith. It describes him as a "friend of God" (Jas. 2:23). In Isaiah 41:8, God says to Israel, "But you, Israel, are My servant, Jacob whom I have chosen, the descendants of Abraham *My friend.*" God Himself considered Abraham His friend. Because of this foundation of friendship, God wouldn't withhold His secrets from Abraham. He shared with Abraham His heart, and it led to intercession for a city.

I have found that intercession is most effective and most sustainable when it is a conversation between friends. That doesn't mean that you should interact with God casually and irreverently. (Abraham certainly didn't do that.) What I mean is that *intercession from a place of friendship and fellowship with God engages your heart differently than when it comes from a place of obligation.*

In 2018, I sensed the Lord commissioning me with a new

assignment in prayer. To be honest, I was hesitant to embrace it. The reason was because I had previously embraced other assignments in prayer, but I was not able to sustain them. They left me weary and disillusioned. Those previous prayer initiatives, though, had not originated from a Spirit-led place, but were rather a result of something else. I had been moved by other people's burdens and made them my own. I felt discouraged by how my passion for them had sputtered out before I saw fruit from my prayers. Therefore, I really weighed this new assignment because I didn't want to repeat the prior cycles of momentary inspiration and then weariness and discouragement. As I pondered it, I sensed the Lord say to me, "I'm looking for a friend to share My heart." Suddenly, revelation flooded my soul about that particular assignment. It was not a bullet point God wanted me to add to a prayer list. It was a burden of His heart, a secret He was looking to share with a friend. Like Abraham, He was inviting me into His counsel to respond with intercession. This intercession would not be an occasional request I hurled at God. It would be an ongoing conversation, at times mixed with tears, at other times filled with revelation—all undergirded by the fellowship and compassion of the Lord.

When you see friendship with God in this way, you realize the watchman call is a call to be available and accessible so God can share the burdens of His heart with you. In the garden of Gethsemane, Jesus wanted the disciples to fulfill this role.

> And He took with Him Peter and the two sons of Zebedee, and He began to be sorrowful and deeply distressed. Then He said to them, "My soul is exceedingly sorrowful, even to death. Stay here and *watch with Me*." He went a little farther and fell on His face and prayed. . . . Then He came to the disciples and found them sleeping, and said to Peter, "What! Could you not *watch with Me* one hour?" (Matthew 26:37–40)

Though most of us remember Jesus charging them, "Watch and

pray," He initially didn't bring up prayer. His first commandment was "watch." Why? His primary concern was not the impact of their prayers, but the fellowship of their presence. It seemed that He simply wanted them with Him during His difficulty and distress. Eventually, Jesus charged them to pray, but He began by telling them, "Watch *with Me*." In this context, watching means to be awake and present while Jesus wrestled in prayer and navigated the sorrow of His own heart. He wanted His disciples to be there as His sweat became great drops of blood. When they fell asleep, He was disappointed that they were not willing to watch with Him.

The garden of Gethsemane gives us a template for the role of a watchman. It is to be awake and attentive to God in the sorrow of His heart. It is to suffer with Him when He suffers and to weep with Him when He weeps. In the garden, Jesus wasn't asking the disciples to pray in order to change the outcome of His betrayal. He was asking them to watch because He wanted His friends with Him in the moment of His distress.

Your prayers certainly do change outcomes and circumstances, but even the power of prayer to change things is not a sustainable foundation for the watchman's lifestyle. *If change is the primary incentive, then you will grow weary when change takes a long time.* You will battle discouragement and the temptation to quit. However, *if friendship is the foundation, then you find joy even in the delay and disappointment because you share that suffering with God Himself.* When we simply want to be with God, then that desire can drive us in intercession for decades because it's an ongoing conversation between intimate friends.

When Jesus found the disciples sleeping, He didn't ask them, "Could you not watch one hour?" He asked, "Could you not *watch with Me* one hour?" The call to be a watchman is the call to be *with Him*. We embrace the vocation of a watchman because God Himself is a watchman, and He wants to share that vocation with us.

God, the Watchman

For years, Psalm 16 has been a chapter that has spoken deeply to my wife and me. Recently, I revisited the psalm to meditate upon its verses, and I noticed something about the watchmen within it that previously escaped me. It begins, "Preserve me, O God, for in You I put my trust." The first word arrested me. I had never particularly considered it. However, a footnote in my Bible explains that "preserve" can also be translated "watch over." Since the watchmen themes are usually in my mind, the footnote piqued my curiosity and provoked me to investigate further.

"Preserve" is the Hebrew word *šāmar*, and it means "to hedge about (as with thorns) . . . ."[2] It carries the strong imagery of protecting and guarding something or someone. It is used frequently in Scripture, 469 times, and it is translated into words such as *keep, observe, heed, keeper, preserve, beware, mark, wait, regard,* and *save*. Fifteen times it is translated as either "watch" or "watchman." Several of the most notable watchmen scriptures use this word. For example, one of the most famous watchmen verses, Isaiah 62:6, used *šāmar* to describe who God had established on the walls of Jerusalem: "I have set *watchmen* [*šāmar*] on your walls, O Jerusalem." It's also found in Psalm 130:6 to describe the watchmen who waited for the morning. Therefore, when Psalm 16:1 used *šāmar* as a prayer to God, it wasn't simply asking for preservation or protection. The psalmist was asking God to personally be his watchman.

Psalm 121 took this concept a step further, though, because it didn't just *ask* God to be a watchman, but it *declared* that is who He is. In only five verses, *šāmar* shows up six times:

He will not allow your foot to be moved; He who *keeps* you will not slumber. Behold, He who *keeps* Israel shall neither slumber nor sleep. The LORD is your *keeper;* the LORD is your shade at your right hand. The sun shall not strike you by day, nor the moon by night. The LORD shall *preserve* you from all evil; He shall *preserve* your soul. The LORD shall *preserve* your going out and your coming in from this time forth, and even forevermore. (Psalm 121:3–8)

As Israel's watchman, the Lord keeps and preserves her by remaining vigilant, not allowing His eyes to sleep. This reference to the Lord's wakefulness is a clear connection to the watchman's vocation. While ancient cities slept, the watchmen stayed awake to guard the cities from potential attacks. In this psalm, God Himself is the Watchman, guarding slumbering Israel. Thus, because God Himself is a watchman, His call to us is not a call to fulfill something simply on behalf of Him, but *with Him*. To say, "God is looking for watchmen," is also to say, "God is looking for friends." He is looking for those who will join Him in wakeful vigilance.

In fact, *the only effective kind of watching is the kind that is done in partnership and friendship with God. Any other kind is fruitless.* Psalm 127 says, "Unless the LORD guards [*šāmar*] the city, the watchman [*šāmar*] stays awake in vain." *We watch because He watches.* Any other endeavor will be fruitless in its impact and unsustainable in its motivation. Attentiveness to prayer requests will not last unless it is a byproduct of attentiveness to God Himself. This call is first and foremost a call to be with God as friends. As Jesus told the disciples, "Watch *with Me*."

CHAPTER FIVE

PROPHETIC SENSITIVITY
(PART 1)

LET'S RETURN TO OUR WORKING DESCRIPTION OF THE WATCHMEN: *In the context of friendship with God, watchmen cultivate prophetic sensitivity, intercessory love, and missional obedience for the sake of cities and nations.* In the last chapter, I described the importance of friendship with God. Now, let's look closer at *prophetic sensitivity.*

In the lifestyle of being a watchman, having a prophetic element to your life is not a luxury. It is a necessity. It is something that must pervade your mind, shape your prayers, and guide your decisions. *A prophetic call and a watchman call are inseparable.* If you don't understand the watchman's prophetic vocation, then you are in danger of misinterpreting and misapplying this assignment. Later in this chapter and the next, I'll explain that some more, but for now let's start by covering the basics of prophetic sensitivity.

There are two sides to the coin of prophetic sensitivity, and both are crucial to properly understanding the call of the watchman. First, the watchman must have a biblical worldview. Before God told Ezekiel to watch, He told Ezekiel to eat. More specifically, He told Ezekiel to eat the scroll: "Moreover He said to me, 'Son of man, eat what you find; eat this scroll, and go, speak to the house of Israel'" (Ezek. 3:1). Before Ezekiel could watch, before he could speak, he must eat *what was written* to give him the right framework of thought to see and speak on behalf of God. *As watchmen, we need to eat, to digest what is written in Scripture.* If we neglect Scripture, then we will lack a proper worldview. We won't have the right lens through which to interpret what God shows in the Spirit and what we see in the world around us.

Scripture gives definition and interpretation to the raw sensory experiences of our eyes and ears. The Gospel of Matthew is a good example of how Scripture enables you to rightly interpret what you see. As Matthew wrote the story of Jesus, he frequently inserted Old Testament scriptures, using the phrase "that it might be fulfilled."* This was not merely Matthew's apologetics. He didn't do this just to prove Jesus was the Messiah to his Jewish audience. Matthew did this to amplify the *meaning* of the story he was telling. *When something happened and Matthew connected it to an Old Testament scripture, suddenly the event resonated within a larger framework and elevated it to cosmic significance.* Thus, when Jesus rode into Jerusalem on a donkey, it wasn't some odd means of transportation. Jesus's riding on a donkey into Jerusalem was a prophecy from Zechariah happening in Matthew's day in surprising ways. When the religious leaders used the blood money from Judas to buy a field, it was the continuation of a story from Jeremiah that had massive significance for Israel and God's promises to her. Matthew amplified and defined these details because he saw them through a biblical lens.

In Acts 2, the apostle Peter did the same thing on the day of Pentecost. The Holy Spirit manifested in unexpected ways: a rushing, mighty wind; tongues of fire; and new wine. The crowds in Jerusalem were perplexed by what they saw as they were not sure how to interpret it. Peter gave meaning to their sensory experience by quoting Scripture:

So they were all amazed and perplexed, saying to one another,

---

* See Matt. 1:22; 2:15, 23; 4:14; 8:17; 12:17; 13:35; 21:4; 27:35

"Whatever could this mean?" Others mocking said, "They are full of new wine." But Peter, standing up with the eleven, raised his voice and said to them, "Men of Judea and all who dwell in Jerusalem . . . this is what was spoken by the prophet Joel." (Acts 2:12–14, 16)

Peter used what was previously written to guide his hearers into the meaning of the new experience. He added a biblical lens to their eyes.

Conversely, in John's Gospel, you see the negative impact of lacking the right biblical framework. When Mary Magdalene visited the tomb of Jesus on Sunday morning, she was distressed because He wasn't there. She ran to get Peter and John, thinking they would surely know what to do. When they arrived at the tomb, there was a mixed reaction. John saw and believed, but Peter just seemed to stare at the emptiness. Both went to their own homes, leaving Mary to sort through her tears and her questions by herself. The visit from these two apostles was an odd, anticlimactic moment. Why didn't they have more to say to Mary or more explanation to give regarding the tomb? Scripture provides this comment: "For as yet they did not know the Scripture, that He must rise again from the dead" (John 20:9). Peter, John, and Mary didn't know how to interpret what they saw because they did not look at it through the lens of Scripture. They didn't see the empty tomb through the biblical narrative; thus, they remained perplexed by what their eyes beheld.

As watchmen, it's not necessarily our job to answer everyone's questions and theologically explain everything that happens in the world. However, we ought to have a biblically informed way of interacting with the world. *We need to internalize Scripture so that, like Matthew, we're able to see the God-story at work in the world around us.*

Jesus Himself modeled this. Particularly at the painful moments of Jesus's life, He was able to interpret them rightly, using Scripture as His guide. At the Last Supper, Jesus revealed that one of the Twelve would betray Him. The disciples were "exceedingly sorrowful," each of them questioning who it would be (Matt. 26:22). Jesus responded to them, "The Son of Man indeed goes just as it is written of Him" (26:24). *In the face of exceeding sorrow and perplexed hearts, Scripture stabilized Jesus.* What was "written of Him" gave meaning to the painful betrayal of Judas. Furthermore, as Jesus hung upon the cross, Scripture governed His mind. He cried out in agony, "'Eli, Eli, lama sabachthani?' that is, 'My God, My God, why have You forsaken Me?'" (27:46). This cry was not just a sudden outburst of Jesus's emotions. It was a cry first penned in Psalm 22:1. *In His deepest moment of suffering, Jesus quoted Scripture.* In doing so, He invoked the *story* of Psalm 22, which descends into intense darkness and persecution, but ultimately ascends into victory and triumph. Even in His darkest moment of pain, Jesus wasn't blind to God's hand at work because Scripture gave Him sight.

When you equip yourself with Scripture, it's like putting on night vision goggles. To everyone else, it may be night, and visibility may be limited. Yet you're able to see what others can't see. In the darkness, you're able to see light. This is key for you as a watchman because your most crucial watching comes during the night when everyone else is asleep. In spiritually and morally dark moments, the watchman must have eyes to penetrate the darkness and perceive accurately what is happening. Without Scripture, though, the watchman's eyes remain blind.

Jesus not only used Scripture to interpret events for Himself, but He also employed Scripture to guide others into revelation. After His resurrection, Jesus drew near to two disciples who were walking from Jerusalem to Emmaus. They knew all the details of Jesus's life and death. They had heard reports of His resurrection. But they didn't know how to interpret all the information. They were in a state of despair. In response to their despondent mood, Jesus used Scripture to open their eyes: "And beginning at Moses and all the Prophets, He expounded to them in all the Scriptures the things concerning Himself" (Luke 24:27). Eventually, they were able to see Him clearly for themselves and then rightly articulate the story to others. *Scripture was the missing link between information and interpretation.* Once Jesus infused them with a Bible-based understanding, the details took shape into a story that had redemptive meaning.

Without Scripture, the events in our world seem like nothing more than a chaotic succession of circumstances. That can provoke despair. However, Scripture gathers it all into a coherent storyline. That's why Ezekiel, and all watchmen, must eat before they watch. *If the scroll is not in us, then we are not using God's story to frame our world.*

The Whole Counsel of God

Also, we must make sure that we are using all of God's story in Scripture—not just the parts we prefer or like. Notice the nature of the scroll God gave to Ezekiel: "Then He spread it before me; and there was writing on the inside and on the outside, and written on it were lamentations and mourning and woe" (2:10). That doesn't sound like the most pleasant meal: lamentations, mourning, and woe. Yet, when Ezekiel eats the scroll, he wrote, "It was in my mouth like honey in sweetness" (3:3). How was such a difficult message sweet in his mouth? *When you have a true prophetic appetite, God's words are sweet even when they're hard to digest.* Proverbs 27:7 says, "A satisfied soul loathes the honeycomb, but to a hungry soul every bitter thing is sweet." When you're hungry to hear from God, it doesn't matter what He says to you as long as He speaks. The "bitter thing" can still taste like a sweet thing. In Revelation, John had a similar experience to that of Ezekiel's:

> Then the voice which I heard from heaven spoke to me again and said, "Go, take the little book which is open in the hand of the angel who stands on the sea and on the earth." So I went to the

angel and said to him, "Give me the little book." And he said to me, "Take and eat it; and it will make your stomach bitter, but it will be as sweet as honey in your mouth." Then I took the little book out of the angel's hand and ate it, and it was as sweet as honey in my mouth. But when I had eaten it, my stomach became bitter. And he said to me, "You must prophesy again about many peoples, nations, tongues, and kings." (Revelation 10:8–11)

When John ate the book, it was sweet as honey, yet it was bitter in his stomach. In other words, the message God gave him was sweet to hear even though the words were hard to digest. This is a key part of prophetic sensitivity. God's words—all of God's words —must be sweet to our taste even when they are hard to digest. *We must have an appetite for anything and everything that comes from God's mouth.* We can't screen out the difficult bits and only see, hear, and say the parts we like or the parts that make us popular.

Paul addressed this temptation when he wrote to his spiritual son, Timothy. He charged him, "Preach the word!" (2 Tim. 4:2). As a young leader, Timothy needed a father to remind him to preach the entirety of God's Word, using his influence to deliver what God says. What is the alternative to preaching the entirety of God's Word? Paul explained, "For the time will come when they will not endure sound doctrine, but according to their own desires, because they have itching ears, they will heap up for themselves teachers; and they will turn their ears away from the truth, and be turned aside to fables" (2 Tim. 4:3–4). If we don't eat the scroll and preach the Word, we will fall into the category of teachers who scratch "itching ears." That means giving people only what they want to hear. It means delivering messages "according to their own desires"—not according to God's desires. Our content will not be watchmen-based messages, but popularity-based messages, which ultimately end not in truth, but in "fables."

To guard against this slide, Paul charged Timothy in the next verse, "But you be *watchful* in *all things*" (4:5). As a leader, Timothy had to have a watchman element to his life. He had to stay vigilant with prophetic sensitivity, which began as biblical saturation and attentiveness. He had to embrace, digest, and teach the full story of Scripture. That's why Paul told him to be watchful in "all things." Not some things. All things.

Paul was able to give Timothy this charge because Paul lived it first himself. In Acts 20, Paul addressed the elders in Ephesus one final time. He knew this would be the last face-to-face meeting with them. He reviewed their story together and the investment he had made into them in order to give them a template for their own leadership. During this review, he said, "For I have not shunned to declare to you the whole counsel of God" (20:27). Paul's ministry included "the whole counsel of God." It wasn't the partial counsel or the popular counsel, but the *whole* counsel of God that he declared. Furthermore, he expected the Ephesian elders to do the same.

This verse also reveals the temptation Paul faced. He said he had "not *shunned*." To shun something is to avoid it and conveniently neglect it. Saying he didn't *shun* the whole counsel of God was an indicator that he was tempted to do exactly that. As individual disciples and as church leaders, it's so easy to avoid the parts of Scripture we don't like or don't understand. Only when we eat the whole scroll—the whole book, everything written "on the inside and on the outside"—can we "prophesy again." Like Ezekiel, like John, the Word of God must come *into* our mouths if we want the word of God to come *out* of our mouths.

CHAPTER SIX

PROPHETIC SENSITIVITY
(PART 2)

A BIBLICAL WORLDVIEW IS THE FIRST STEP TOWARD PROPHETIC sensitivity. The second step is *disciplined silence*. Ezekiel lived both.

Ezekiel 3:16–21 is the most well-known passage that describes the vocation of a watchman. It emphasizes the *vocal* mandate the watchman carries to warn others of impending judgment. Yet you rarely hear about the rest of the chapter where God described to Ezekiel his *silent* mandate:

> Then the Spirit entered me and set me on my feet, and spoke with me and said to me: "Go, shut yourself inside your house. And you, O son of man, surely they will put ropes on you and bind you with them, so that you cannot go out among them. I will make your tongue cling to the roof of your mouth, so that you shall be mute and not be one to rebuke them, for they are a rebellious house." (Ezekiel 3:24–26)

This commandment to be silent is quite odd for someone called to be a prophet, warning others of approaching death. God told Ezekiel to shut himself inside his house. Then, someone would bind him there with ropes. (It isn't clear who these people were that would bind him. Could it have been other men? Or possibly angels?) Furthermore, if isolation and seclusion were not enough, God would physically restrict Ezekiel's mouth to keep him mute and silent. The purpose, God explained, was to restrain Ezekiel from rebuking the house of Israel.

If you compare verses 24–26 to the passage that precedes them, they are incongruent. One passage told Ezekiel to speak and the other to shut his mouth. Furthermore, it seems contradictory to the rest of Ezekiel's book, which contains extended sections of rebuking Israel. If Ezekiel's vocation was to be vocal and if Ezekiel's message carried a rebuke, then why did God restrict his speech and tell him not to rebuke?

The answer is found in the next verse: "But *when I speak with you*, I will open your mouth, and you shall say to them, 'Thus says the Lord GOD. . .'" (3:27). God imposed silence upon Ezekiel *until* Ezekiel heard God's voice. God restricted Ezekiel to isolation *until* Ezekiel received the Lord's counsel. God did not want Ezekiel to speak in a reactionary way, based upon the condition or actions of the people. God wanted Ezekiel to minister solely based upon the word of the Lord.

This is what I mean by *disciplined silence.* To be a watchman is to watch. It is to wait upon the Lord in silence and seclusion until He speaks. Then, you react based upon what God reveals. You respond with prophetic sensitivity. *If we only embrace the vocal call of the watchman without embracing the silent call of the watchman, we will misinterpret and misapply what it means to be a watchman.* We must wait upon the Lord for His counsel and then pray, act, and speak from what we hear God say.

If we don't cultivate prophetic sensitivity, then we will become social commentators rather than watchmen. What is the difference? A social commentator observes the behaviors of the world around him, the trends and patterns of society, and then responds based upon his own assessment of what he sees there. Though his assessment may be accurate because it is based upon empirical evidence, that doesn't mean it contains the word of the Lord for the situation. Thus, his response is only commentary without any real prescription for transformation. Only the word of the Lord can bring conviction and repentance. *The word of man may rebuke with righteous zeal, but if it remains the word of man alone, then it only becomes white noise.*

God restrained Ezekiel from rebuking Israel not because Israel didn't need to be rebuked. He restrained Ezekiel from rebuking Israel until Ezekiel could rebuke her in the name of the Lord rather than in his own name. This is one application of God's commandment, "You shall not take the name of the LORD your God in vain" (Deut. 5:11). *God doesn't want His prophets to take His name and vainly add it to their own words.* God knew that if He did not restrain Ezekiel, then Ezekiel would have observed Israel's actions and rebuked her out of his own zealous heart. Though a heart be zealous, its words do not always benefit the hearers. Therefore, God isolated and silenced the prophet until the prophet gained the mind of the Lord on the matter.

The vocation to silence first is one of the most needed mandates for leaders today. We are surrounded by an abundance of platforms where our voices can be heard. We are also surround by an abundance of informants about the behaviors of the world around us. If we are not diligent to slow down and listen to God, then we will rebuke in a reactionary way. That kind of rebuke does not produce change in its hearers. Consider James 1:19–20: "So then, my beloved brethren, let every man be swift to hear, slow to speak, slow to wrath; for the wrath of man does not produce the righteousness of God." We typically think of this verse in terms of personal relationships. What if we applied it to the public platforms in our lives? The first responsibility is not to speak, but to hear. From that patient place of watching and waiting upon God, we gain the words that can produce "the righteousness of God" in the situations and the lives around us.

Ran, but Not Sent

Jeremiah 23 outlines the detrimental consequences of leaders who speak their words rather than God's words. The situation was quite bleak: "For the land is full of adulterers; for because of a curse the land mourns. The pleasant places of the wilderness are dried up. Their course of life is evil, and their might is not right" (Jer. 23:10). This condition of rampant sin stemmed from the failure of the prophets to hear and deliver the word of the Lord. Before Jeremiah wept for the land, he wept for the prophets and for the Lord's words that were falling on deaf ears. He wrote, "My heart within me is broken because of the prophets . . . because of the LORD, and because of His holy words" (23:9). As a prophet himself who heard, carried, and delivered God's word, he was brokenhearted by the misrepresentation of the other "prophets." They were certainly speaking, but they did not represent the Lord or "His holy words." According to Jeremiah 23:16, "They speak a vision of their own heart, not from the mouth of the LORD." Their words originate from their own heart and not from God's. The result is that wickedness not only persists in the land, but increases more and more. "'For from the prophets of Jerusalem profaneness has gone out into all the land'" (23:15).

The first time I ever read this chapter, it provoked the fear of the Lord within me as a leader. I never wanted my life and message to have the same result, leading people to sin. I never wanted God to say about me what He said about them: "I have not sent these prophets, yet they ran. I have not spoken to them, yet they prophesied" (23:21). As I read it, I found myself asking these questions, "How can I ensure that I don't speak a vision of my own heart? How can I avoid giving people my words rather than the Lord's words?" Thankfully, as I continued to read Jeremiah 23, I realized that it not only identifies the problem, but it also prescribes the solution: "But if they [the prophets] had stood in My counsel, and had caused My people to hear My words, then they would have turned them from their evil way and from the evil of their doings" (23:22). The answer to this dire situation was rather simple. The prophets only had to stand in the Lord's counsel. If they had stood in His counsel, waiting to hear His words, then they could have spoken His counsel and caused others to hear His words. God's words would have turned the people "from their evil way." God's words would have brought repentance and life. Unfortunately, though, very few leaders were willing to wait and hear God speak. This lack of listening leaders caused God to ask, "For who has stood in the counsel of the LORD, and has perceived and heard His word?" (23:18). *It is essential to wait on His counsel, perceive His directives, and hear His word.*

Embrace Boredom

Thus, silence must precede oration. It's worth noting that a watchman is called a *watch*man. The primary call is watching, not speaking. It includes speaking, but most of his job description is to watch. This requires a certain discipline of the mind to embrace boredom. *Watching and waiting upon the Lord may not always be the most exciting, stimulating activity.* If you think about watchmen in ancient cities, most of their days were likely uneventful. With their eyes on the horizon, they would remain vigilant, whether anything approached the city. In the same way, watchmen in the Spirit must learn vigilance even in boring periods of waiting. Otherwise, our impatience will drive us to hasty speech that may not be filled with the Lord's counsel.

This embrace of boredom emphasizes how important it is for friendship with the Lord to be the foundation of the watchman's lifestyle. If speaking on behalf of God is the primary motivation, then we will have difficulty waiting when we're not hearing anything. On the other hand, if the motivation is friendship, then we're much more likely to wait in the silence because we simply want to be with Him.

I was particularly inspired by a message from Corey Russell on this topic. He described an experience he had that demonstrates how much God is looking for friends and not just messengers. One night, he sensed the Lord waking him three different times. Corey explained how unusual that was because he is such a heavy sleeper. Eventually, he got up to pray, expecting God to give him some type of revelation or word. *If God woke me up, then surely He had something important to say,* Corey thought to himself. After praying for a while, Corey didn't hear or sense anything specific. Discouraged, he went back to bed. The next day, he described the experience to a friend. Corey asked, "Did I do something wrong? I thought God wanted to speak to me." The friend responded, "You didn't do anything wrong at all. God just wanted to be with you."

I love this story because it's a good description of a watchman rhythm. It's not just about seeing and hearing. It's waiting in the place of friendship with God. Eventually, though, in that place of friendship, God wants to share His heart and reveal His counsel. Before we speak on behalf of God, it's important to know that we've heard from God.

A well-known verse for church leaders is Habakkuk 2:2: "Then the LORD answered me and said: 'Write the vision and make it plain on tablets that he may run who reads it.'" Leaders love this verse because it gives a clear leadership principle. Before the people around you can run with confidence, they need to clearly understand the vision you carry. Therefore, write it and make it plain. Though we love this verse, most of the time we overlook the verse that precedes it. It says, "I will stand my watch and set myself on the rampart, and watch to see what He will say to me, and what I will answer when I am corrected" (2:1). Before Habakkuk heard from the Lord to write the vision, he first set himself to watch. He set himself to wait "to see what He will say." *Without watching, waiting, seeing, and hearing, there is no vision to write—at least, not a vision from the Lord.* Habakkuk could clarify a vision for people to run because he had first seen a vision from the Lord. If we're not careful to take the preliminary step of watching, then we're in danger of fulfilling the words God spoke in Jeremiah 23:21: "I have not sent these prophets, yet they ran." *Just because we run doesn't mean we're carrying the Lord's message to others.*

The call to watch before we speak is summarized perfectly in Isaiah 21:6: "For thus has the Lord said to me: 'Go, set a watchman, let him declare what he sees.'"

Yes, the vocation of the watchman includes declaration. It begins, though, with setting yourself to see. If you don't see something, then you have nothing to declare. And if you don't set yourself to watch, then you won't ever see. This emphasizes my original point in the chapter. *Prophetic sensitivity is not a luxury for the watchman. It is a necessity.* God bound Ezekiel in Ezekiel's house and closed his mouth *until* Ezekiel heard from God. Speaking God's word is an imperative, and speaking His word requires hearing His word.

Silence Requires Humility

This requires not only patience in the face of boredom, but also humility in the face of silence. *If we are to grow beyond mere social commentary and truly become watchmen, then we need to embrace the fact that we will not always have something to say.* This is difficult for our pride because, when we are silent, it may also appear that we are ignorant. It may appear as though we are uninformed or uneducated about the world around us. When we're tempted to feel this way, we need to recall the image of Ezekiel's shut mouth. God made Ezekiel's tongue cling to the roof of his mouth so that he wouldn't speak outside of the parameters of the Lord's counsel.

When the Lord first gave me the watchmen dream, I felt quite intimidated by the prophetic aspect of this vocation. It was during the COVID-19 global pandemic, and there was quite a bit of social commentary floating around the Church. As I continued to hear the call of God to cultivate prophetic sensitivity, I had a hard time visualizing myself as someone who could do that. Thankfully, the Holy Spirit interrupted me and reshaped my understanding of the prophetic. He told me, "To be prophetic is not to be omniscient. It is to hear what the Father is saying to you." This statement immediately liberated my heart. I realized that a prophetic gift doesn't mean that you have something to say about everything. It means *intentional silence except about the things God reveals.* Furthermore, to be a prophet doesn't always equal a prolific output of content. Yes, there are certain prophets, like Isaiah, who release chapters upon chapters of the word of the Lord. There are also prophets, like Obadiah, who release a handful of verses. We must be humble enough to be an Obadiah if that is how God speaks to us. Most of the time, though, our pride aspires to be an Isaiah, and we go beyond the words God gives us just for the sake of having something to say.

We need to keep reminding ourselves about disciplined silence as we grow as watchmen. It's not just relevant for initially embracing the call, but also sustaining the call. In fact, it may be *more* relevant for those who have some experience behind them. Once you speak something prophetically and accurately, people will then ascribe credibility to your words. With that comes an expectation that you will do it again—release another prophetic word that they can trust. The expectation can induce pressure to say something—anything—especially when you have a platform created by your previous prophetic ministry. When you're quiet, it can disappoint your audience. Disappointing your audience, however, would be much better than misleading them by using your own words and ascribing them to God's mouth. *Infrequent but integrous ministry is better than frequent words that are nothing more than profitless noise.*

When we speak just for the sake of speaking rather than because we carry a message, then we suddenly become watchdogs rather that watchmen. What is the difference? *Watchdogs make a lot of noise, but there is no discernible message within their bark. Furthermore, they tend to bark at everything.* Whether it's good, bad, dangerous, or friendly, watchdogs react based upon their territorial instincts. It could be the mailman, a friend, or a burglar that provokes them. Though they may be valuable in raising an alert, no one knows what to do based solely upon their noise. In the same way, our chronic social commentary may make a lot of noise and raise a degree of awareness, but it doesn't guide the Church with legitimate counsel. *Watchmen are distinct from watchdogs because they have the capacity to form words. They can describe what they see and give intelligent feedback about what they have heard.*

A Higher Plane of Counsel

It's imperative to move beyond social observation into our prophetic vocation. Anyone can observe cultural trends and respond to them. Only the sons and daughters of God can access His counsel and release it through prayer and prophecy. Furthermore, if we remain solely in the realm of social observation, then we will most likely miss the topics God wants to emphasize. If we only live within the realm that we can see, then we'll miss the unseen realities that God wants to show us.

As you grow as a watchman, you may be surprised when the things on God's mind are not always the same things on your mind. In other words, *God is not always thinking about the things we think He's thinking about.* Our minds are conditioned by the world around us to meditate on certain things. Social media algorithms and news cycles prioritize content for us and, thus, determine our focus. We automatically assume God has something to say about all of it. Of course, God does have something to say about everything, but just because a story is getting a lot of press coverage doesn't mean it's the primary thing God wants to talk to us about. Sometimes, it is. Sometimes, it's not. *Part of the danger of merely being a social observer is that we get out of rhythm with God because we are wholly in rhythm with the spirit of the age.* Again, God may surprise you with the things on His mind.

This was certainly true for Ezekiel. On one hand, God had a lot to say about the condition of the people directly in front of Ezekiel. He talked to Ezekiel about their sin, their waywardness, and their need for repentance. On the other hand, God also talked to Ezekiel about something else. God talked to him about something that was not a response to the sin of the people, but was a vision of better days to come. Amid devastation and destruction, God talked about a future day when a glorious temple will stand again in Jerusalem. The last nine chapters (40–48) are dedicated wholly to this vision, describing in detail dimensions of the buildings and the renovation of the city. I would assume this last section of Ezekiel's book came as a surprise to him. I would assume that, left to himself, Ezekiel would not have ventured into wondrous descriptions of a redeemed and renewed temple. Most likely, he would not have gone beyond the very natural reaction of his anger to Israel's rebellion.

This vision of the new temple played an important role. God told Ezekiel, "Son of man, describe the temple to the house of Israel, that they may be ashamed of their iniquities" (43:10). Oddly enough, it's not just the rebukes that caused Israel to be ashamed of her sin. It was also the promise of restoration. When the people saw how God planned to redeem them and rebuild them, the promise of a glorious future induced embarrassment for their present condition.

If we only respond to the condition of the world as we see it with our natural eyes, we'll never go beyond soulish interpretations and reactions. We'll never see from a higher plane of promises and God's glorious future. Thus, we reinforce the condition in front of us by only *speaking to it* instead of *about it* from the standpoint of God's redemptive plan. When you wait on God and watch for His word, He surprises you with what He reveals.

Watchman watch until they see. Certainly, they declare what they see, but first, they must see. As God told Ezekiel, "Declare to the house of Israel *everything you see*" (Ezek. 40:4).

CHAPTER SEVEN
INTERCESSORY LOVE

LET'S NOW RETURN TO THE STRATEGIC ROLE THAT WATCHMEN PLAY regarding cities. So far, I have described non-spatial components that can be applied anywhere and by anyone: holy interruption, friendship with God, and prophetic sensitivity. Each of those are principle-based, but the watchman vocation is not principle-based alone. The assignment is locale minded. It is connected to specific people and places.

You find this connection to geography in our working definition of the watchman: In the context of friendship with God, watchmen cultivate prophetic sensitivity, intercessory love, and missional obedience *for the sake of cities and nations*. I include "cities *and* nations" because their sphere of intercession and responsibility can grow beyond one city to include multiple cities, entire regions, and even nations. The word *nations* also embodies the idea of specific people groups. Regardless of the exact assignment of each watchman, that assignment will undoubtedly include a deep connection to a physical place on the earth and the people who live there, which leads to the next characteristic I want to describe: *intercessory love*.

We must not overlook the importance of loving the cities for which we watch, or our development as watchmen will then be incomplete. It's not enough to simply see something prophetically and then vocally declare what we see. We must see, *engage in prayer*, and then release the word of the Lord from hearts of compassion. The prophets in Scripture were not just trumpets, thundering the voice of the Lord. They were also men and women of compassion, and their eyes were conduits for God's tears. *The prophets wept for the cities to which they prophesied.*

Jeremiah may be the most notable of these weeping prophets. When he saw destruction coming for the city of Jerusalem and the children of Israel, he was not indifferent. He reacted with intense emotion and sorrow.

> For the hurt of the daughter of my people I am hurt. I am mourning; astonishment has taken hold of me. . . . Oh, that my head were waters, and my eyes a fountain of tears, that I might weep day and night for the slain of the daughter of my people! . . . I will take up a weeping and wailing for the mountains, and for the dwelling places of the wilderness a lamentation. (Jeremiah 8:21; 9:1, 10)

When Jerusalem was hurt, Jeremiah was hurt. When Jerusalem wept, Jeremiah wept. When Jerusalem was slain, Jeremiah's own heart was slain. *The prophet's call to the city wasn't an emotionally detached work assignment. His call was a covenantal identification with the people and the land.* When Jeremiah prayed that he "might weep day and night," it wasn't because he had difficultly feeling compassion and needed help weeping. He prayed that because he had already cried his tears dry, and he was asking God for the ability to continue to express his sorrow physically through unending tears. In this frame of mind, Jeremiah wrote the book of Lamentations. In it, he revealed not just the destruction of the city, but the destruction of the prophet who loved the city. Jeremiah saw his own destiny entwined with the destiny of Jerusalem.

Though Jeremiah is the most notable among the biblical prophets for his tears, he is certainly not alone. The other prophets also wept for the cities to which they prophesied. They saw what was coming, reacted emotionally, and contended with God concerning their destinies. The prophet Micah certainly embodied this blend of prophetic insight, compassionate tears, and intercessory engagement. Before he named the nine cities that I learned about in my dream, Micah described first how he felt about their impending doom: "Therefore I will wail and howl, I will go stripped and naked; I will make a wailing like the jackals and a mourning like the ostriches" (1:8).

Micah did not take pleasure in the destruction of the nine cities. When he saw it, he wailed to such a degree that it made him look like beasts, like a jackal and an ostrich. Furthermore, the way Micah described the cities revealed the kind of affection he had for them. Butler calls it "warm familiarity" (469). Micah didn't just call them by name and say that judgment was coming. He used their names and the meanings of their names to describe what kind of judgment was coming (and for two of them, the kind of promises that were beyond the judgment). He was so familiar with these cities that he understood their identities, their potential, their faults, the results of their sins, and what it looked like for them to step into promises. Micah knew these cities. He understood them in natural, poetic, and prophetic dimensions.

Like Micah, do we know our cities in these ways? Do we understand the natural dynamics of our cities, knowing their histories and cultures? Do we have a sense of their poetic flavor, identifying with their beauties and sorrows? Are we tapped into their prophetic dimensions, knowing the word of the Lord and the spiritual currents coursing through their atmospheres? All these factors contribute to the watchmen's intercessory lifestyle. Watchmen do not just reside within cities. They love cities and feel a sense of ownership for them. Ezekiel felt this for Jerusalem, even when he lived in exile from the city. Your love and intercession for a city is not wholly dependent upon living within it. God can initiate a supernatural love in your heart, even when there is distance between you and that place. *Being a watchman is not primarily about residence, but ownership.*

Adopting Cities

When I said in my dream, "God is looking for watchmen, or cities will be no more," I knew that God is looking for people who will take spiritual responsibility for cities. He is looking for people who will spiritually adopt them. This idea of spiritually adopting a city may seem odd, but Scripture gives us precedent for it.

At the beginning of 1 Chronicles, there are quite a few genealogies. While they are not always the most enjoyable to read, they certainly have value, and they are a part of the canon of inspired Scripture. If you read them closely, you'll discover quite a few gems within their lists. First Chronicles 2:50–51 are two verses that contain some of those gems: "These were the descendants of Caleb: The sons of Hur, the firstborn of Ephrathah, were Shobal the father of Kirjath Jearim, Salma the father of Bethlehem, and Hareph the father of Beth Gader." After listing the succession of descendants from fathers to sons, these verses do something a little different. They list Shobal, Salma, and Hareph not as the fathers of sons, but as the fathers of cities. Kirjath Jearim, Bethlehem, and Beth Gader are not people. They are cities. (Sometimes, the names of people later become cities, but that is not the case with these three.) What is the point I'm making? Just like someone can be the father or mother of an individual, someone can also be the father or mother of a city. Of course, these three men probably founded these cities and became their fathers in that way. However, when you adopt someone, you take responsibility for that person, though you didn't birth them. In the same way, we can take responsibility for cities we didn't found or birth if we become caretakers for their spiritual condition. As watchmen, that is what we do. *We take responsibility for the cities God gives us with the heart of a father or mother. We refuse to be indifferent, and we think of these cities as our own.*

Jeremiah, Micah, and the other prophets all model for us the kind of ownership and compassion God is looking for within His watchmen. He wants us to love cities. This is the standard heart posture of the prophets. When that is absent, we may carry an accurate description of God's Word, but we won't reveal an accurate depiction of God's heart. We can see that danger in the life and ministry of Jonah, who was an exception to the city-loving prophets.

Prophecies, but Not Tears

Jonah was an accurate prophetic voice, yet he prophesied to a city he did not love. When God told Jonah to go to Nineveh, Jonah was clearly not enthused. He took extreme measures to resist what God told him to do. It's interesting that Scripture says, "Jonah arose to flee to Tarshish from the presence of the LORD" (Jon. 1:3). Notice that it doesn't say he fled from his assignment or from the city of Nineveh. It says he fled "from the presence of the LORD." This reinforces the idea that friendship with God is the foundation of the watchman assignment. God's call to Jonah was not just the call to be a prophet to a wayward city. It was the call to fresh friendship with God where He could share with Jonah the sorrows and secrets of His heart. *When Jonah refused the assignment, he was saying, "No," to deeper friendship with God.*

Eventually, Jonah went to Nineveh, and he prophesied. Though reluctant, his ministry was so effective that the entire city responded in repentance through fasting and prayer. God then relented from His judgment and extended mercy to the city. With such a dramatic turn of events, you would expect Jonah to rejoice, but that was not the case. His heart was cold toward the people, and he was more concerned for his own preferences and comfort than their existential crisis. As I stated earlier, the problem was Jonah prophesied to a city he did not love. He ministered to a city for which he had no tears.

You may wonder if Jonah had difficulty with compassion overall. Perhaps, this was a part of Jonah's makeup. Perhaps, he was not prone toward mercy and gravitated toward a sense of retribution, seeing people get what they deserved. The only problem with that theory is Scripture gives us a different view of him. Before the book of Jonah, we're introduced to him earlier in Scripture, and it revealed he had a tendency to embrace mercy.

Second Kings 14 introduces us to Jonah during the reign of Jeroboam II. What were the conditions in Israel during Jeroboam's reign? Well, they were far from perfect. According to 2 Kings 14:24, "[Jeroboam II] did evil in the sight of the LORD; he did not depart from all the sins of Jeroboam the son of Nebat, who had made Israel sin." Jeroboam II personally continued in the sins of the first Jeroboam, which became a cultural stronghold in the nation.

To consolidate and preserve his power as king, Jeroboam I made two golden calves, putting one in the south of his kingdom at Bethel and one in the north at Dan (see 1 Kings 12:26–33). Then, he discouraged the people from going to Jerusalem to worship, lest they turned their hearts back to the house of David. In addition to the two golden calves, he also built pagan shrines on the high places throughout Samaria. He then profaned the priesthood by consecrating non-Levites as priests. Finally, he established his own "sacred" feast in Bethel to rival the feasts appointed by the Lord in Jerusalem. The result was perpetual idolatry in the land of Israel for generations. Jeroboam II continued this multifaceted, multidimensional sin that the first Jeroboam began.

It was in this setting that God commissioned Jonah as a prophet. Given what we know about Jonah from the episode in Nineveh, you would expect him to have delivered a word of judgment, directly confronting the sins of the king and the nation. After all, when Jeroboam son of Nebat began this pattern of idolatry, God spoke clearly about the judgment it would invoke (see 1 Kings 13:1–3; 14:1–18). The prophets declared destruction upon the altar, the priests, and the house of Jeroboam. They declared to Israel that God would strike, uproot, scatter, and give her up. Knowing that history, you would assume Jonah would have delivered a similar message to Jeroboam II. That's not quite what happened, though.

During Jeroboam II's reign, God surprisingly worked within Israel constructively rather than destructively. Second Kings 14:25 says that Jeroboam II "restored the territory of Israel from the entrance of Hamath to the Sea of Arabah." Rather than subtraction of land, there was restoration of land. This restoration was not mere happenstance, as the rest of the verse explains that this happened "according to the word of the LORD God of Israel." Amid the people's sin, God worked among them mercifully and kindly, according to His word. Furthermore, 2 Kings 14:25 explains through whom this word came, saying that God "had spoken through His servant Jonah the son of Amittai." Thus, Jonah was the instrument of God's mercy. He prophesied about the Lord's tender mercies, despite the longstanding pagan worship in the land. You find the compassionate motive behind Jonah's ministry captured in the next verse: "For the LORD saw that the affliction of Israel was very bitter; and whether bond or free, there was no helper for Israel." Though their own sin had carried them into bitter affliction, God chose to respond in forbearance and love. God displayed radical mercy through His prophet Jonah.

With this in mind, it's no wonder that God chose Jonah as His prophet to go to Nineveh. He had another mission of radical mercy in mind. He wanted to respond to another wayward, pagan people with forbearance and love. He wanted to extend grace to a city that did not deserve it. Jonah had been this kind of instrument before, and he should have been ready to do it again. This time, though, Jonah had a problem with God's plan.

Jonah was willing to respond in compassion when the assignment included cities within his nation, but he was unwilling when the assignment took him elsewhere, especially into the Assyrian Empire. Nineveh was the capital of the Assyrian Empire, which decimated the Northern Kingdom of Israel. Because of the natural conflict of interest, Jonah's heart was calloused regarding the Ninevites. Eventually, he reluctantly prophesied to the city, but he never loved it.

What is the application for us as watchmen? It's not enough to simply love the cities for which we already have a warm familiarity. God wants to expand our hearts to love cities that are foreign and potentially hostile to us. God wants us to have a supernatural love for cities, a love that comes from His heart. If we don't receive a supernatural love from God, then we'll be limited by our own human capacity. We'll be limited by our own preferences. To be a watchman is not to go and pray and watch only where you have a preference. On the contrary, it is to go, pray, and watch in the places God has revealed to you within the secret place of friendship with Him. In fact, *if we base our assignments upon our natural preferences, we are in danger of becoming soulish-based commentators rather than Spirit-led watchmen.* We should not adopt cities just because we like their vibe, but because the Spirit of God initiated an unmistakable, unshakable heart journey in us.

Jonah loved Israel, so he could prophesy mercy amid idolatry. Though he had the authority to bring change, Jonah did not love Nineveh, so he remained detached from Nineveh's condition and destiny. May we learn from this comparison and ask God to expand our hearts. May we love the cities to which we are called and respond with intercessory compassion when we see destruction on the horizon. *We ought not relish coming judgment but realize that God has revealed it as an invitation to intercession.*

Stand before the LORD

If Jonah's indifference is something we need to avoid, is there a counterexample of someone who should inspire us? Can we find someone who heard from God about judgment and then responded in compassion? The answer is yes. The intercessory instinct and reaction of Abraham should be central to our understanding of the watchman call. His intercession was not just something that touched God when Abraham did it, but it lodged itself in the memory of God, and He looked for it again in the future.

Let's return to Abraham and Sodom in Genesis 18. From that example, we learn about the way friendship gives us access to God's secrets. We also learn how prophetic sensitivity ought to lead to intercession. When God revealed the outcry against Sodom, Abraham didn't take for granted that judgment was certain. Neither was he indifferent to Sodom's condition and future. He was proactive to plead for the city to be spared:

> And the LORD said, "Because the outcry against Sodom and Gomorrah is great, and because their sin is very grave, I will go down now and see whether they have done altogether according to the outcry against it that has come to Me; and if not, I will know." Then the men turned away from there and went toward Sodom, but Abraham still stood before the LORD. (Genesis 18:20–22)

Abraham could have simply let the "men" go assess the city and bring its due punishment. Instead, Abraham "stood before the LORD," and Abraham contended with Him for mercy. This is the first instance found in Scripture of someone standing before the Lord as an intercessor on behalf of others. Because of Abraham's intercession, Sodom could have been spared. God agreed with Abraham's request that He would spare the city if He found ten righteous (see Gen. 18:32). Unfortunately, there were not even ten righteous in the city, so it was destroyed. Its destruction, however, was not a result of Abraham's indifference. He was not absent from his post, leaving Sodom to its fate. Abraham's love for

Sodom and for his relatives who were living there is a beautiful example of intercessory love and standing before the Lord.

Ezekiel 22 emphasizes this crucial role of standing before the Lord as an act of loving and guarding cities. Throughout the chapter, God recounted the sins of Jerusalem and Israel. He described the wicked things they had done and the consequential judgment that was coming. The directness with which God spoke emphasized His anger concerning her persistent sin. Furthermore, His words were emphatic, leaving no doubt about the certainty of coming wrath. That seeming certainty was suddenly brought into question by the last two verses in the chapter, however. At the end of the passage, God revealed that their fate was not pre-determined, but that something could have changed it. What would have changed it? Ezekiel 22:30 says, "I sought for a man among them who would make a wall, and stand in the gap before Me on behalf of the land, that I should not destroy it; but I found no one." This verse is quite profound. After giving an itemized list of all the ways Jerusalem rebelled against Him and a vivid description of the way in which He will judge them for it, God then disclosed a secret about Himself. Amid sin and judgment, He looked for an intercessor who would appeal to His mercy. He looked for a watchman who would "make a wall and stand in the gap" before Him "on behalf of the land." He looked for someone to whom He could show the impending judgment and that one respond with intercession. Because God did not find that person in Ezekiel 22, the judgment finally came: "I found no one. Therefore I have poured out My indignation on them; I have consumed them with the fire of My wrath; and I have recompensed their deeds on their own heads" (22:30–31). If a watchman had been found, his intercession could have diverted God's judgment.

Perhaps, it is Abraham that God had in mind when He said in Ezekiel 22:30 that He sought for someone to "stand . . . before [Him] on behalf of the land." God was looking for another friend with the kind of compassion for Jerusalem that Abraham had for

Sodom. Instead, Jerusalem was destroyed because the watchmen were absent. God could not find an intercessor on her behalf.

The Isaiah 62 Watchmen

Ezekiel 22 gives us a bleak picture of what happened to Jerusalem without watchmen. Isaiah 62, on the other hand, gives us a different picture, showing us what will happen when Israel has watchmen. It's speaking of a future time. Isaiah 62 is a chapter that models the lifestyle of a watchman. It's a chapter we will consider throughout this book because it contains many insights that we need. One facet it reveals is the clear love watchmen have for the city they are guarding.

The Isaiah 62 watchmen of Jerusalem are vigilant, carrying the city within their hearts through fervent intercession. This intercession is so intense that the watchmen do not rest day or night. They contend for the destiny of the city through their prayers. The chapter begins, "For Zion's sake . . . for Jerusalem's sake . . ." (62:1). It is the watchmen's love for the city of Jerusalem that drives them day and night. The watchmen are familiar with her faults, but they are also familiar with her promises. They set themselves to an immovable, unwavering stance of contending prayer until God fulfills His promises to Jerusalem.

Where does this passion for Jerusalem come from? The watchmen's hearts are beating with love for the city because God's heart beats with love for the city. Consider this passage:

You shall no longer be termed Forsaken, nor shall your land any more be termed Desolate; but you shall be called Hephzibah [My Delight Is in Her], and your land Beulah [Married]; for the LORD delights in you, and your land shall be married. For as a young man marries a virgin, so shall your sons marry you; and as the bridegroom rejoices over the bride, so shall your God rejoice over you. (Isaiah 62:4–5)

Because "the LORD delights" in Jerusalem, she shall be "married." She won't just be married by God; she will be married by the sons of the city: "So shall your sons marry you." The idea is that a company of people begin to burn with God's love for the city of Jerusalem, and from that love they will operate in covenantal commitment to her. That covenant love looks like a steadfast commitment to Jerusalem's wellbeing and prophetic destiny. Then, as a company of people love the city, their intercessory love becomes the gateway through which God's own love finds action and expression.

Here is the progression:

- Jerusalem's ultimate destiny is to be married: "You shall no longer be termed Forsaken, nor shall your land any more be termed Desolate; but you shall be called Hephzibah [My Delight Is in Her], and your land Beulah [Married]."
- This originates from God's own desire for the city: "For the LORD delights in you, and your land shall be married."
- God's desire for the city permeates the hearts of the watchmen, and they move into covenantal love for the city themselves: "For as a young man marries a virgin, shall your sons marry you."
- The watchmen's love becomes the gateway through which God's love and promises are fulfilled: "And as the bridegroom rejoices over the bride, so shall your God rejoice over you."

When watchmen love cities, God's love finds a way to those cities. When watchmen do not love cities, those cities remain "Forsaken" and "Desolate." It's not because God doesn't love them. It's because watchmen have left their post of friendship with God and intercession for the city.

The foundation of the watchman's call is friendship with God, and the driving force of the watchman's motivation is love for the city God has given to him or her. In fact, these two things are so intertwined that it's difficult to separate them. Within the context of friendship with God, He shares with you His heart. Because God loves the world, because He loves the people within cities and nations, He shares with you that love. Then, friendship with Him looks like a mutually shared interest.

In J. R. R. Tolkien's *The Lord of the Rings*, there is a character who beautifully exemplifies this love for cities. His name is Faramir, and his father is the Steward of a realm called Gondor. The two cities in that realm closest to his heart are Minas Tirith and Minas Anor. As he describes his responsibility as a watchman and a warrior, his love for the cities and the people in his realm rises to the surface:

> I would see . . . Minas Tirith in peace: Minas Anor again as of old, full of light, high and fair, beautiful as a queen among other queens. . . . War must be, while we defend our lives against a destroyer who would devour all; but I do not love the bright sword for its sharpness, nor the arrow for its swiftness, nor the warrior for his glory. I love only that which they defend: the city of the Men of Númenor; and I would have her loved for her memory, her ancientry, her beauty, and her present wisdom.[1]

Like Faramir, you don't watch because you're simply fulfilling a job. You don't pray and prophesy because you need your voice to be heard. *You fulfill your vocation as a watchman because you love that which you defend—the cities, nations, and people God loves.*

It's not enough for watchmen to simply see what is coming with prophetic sensitivity. They must see what is coming and then respond in intercession. Through prayer, they must become catalysts for promises and intercessors for judgment. This kind of intercessory love shapes the destinies of cities.

CHAPTER EIGHT

MISSIONAL OBEDIENCE

As watchmen gain the counsel of the Lord through prophetic sensitivity and then respond to that counsel through intercessory love, it's important for them to take one more step: *missional obedience.* At some point, *their hearing ears and their weeping eyes must translate into obedient feet.* From the place of prayer, they must emerge with words and actions that display the counsel of the Lord to others.

I call this aspect not just obedience, but *missional* obedience. I use the word *missional* because the watchmen's obedience is not just a personal, private matter of accountability before God (though it does include that), but their obedience has real consequences in the lives of other people. Their obedience matters, and their disobedience matters as well.

When God first spoke to Ezekiel about being a watchman, He started with Ezekiel's missional responsibility toward others:

Son of man, I have made you a watchman for the house of Israel. . . . When I say to the wicked, "You shall surely die," and you give him no warning, nor speak to warn the wicked from his wicked way, to save his life, that same wicked man shall die in his iniquity; but his blood I will require at your hand. Yet, if you warn the wicked, and he does not turn from his wickedness, nor from his wicked way, he shall die in his iniquity; but you have delivered your soul. Again, when a righteous man turns from his right-eousness and commits iniquity, and I lay a stumbling block before him, he shall die; because you did not give him warning, he shall die in his sin, and his righteousness which he has done shall not be remembered; but his blood I will require at your hand. Never-theless if you warn the righteous man that the righteous should not sin, and he does not sin, he shall surely live because he took warning; also you will have delivered your soul. (Ezekiel 3:17–21)

After the whirlwind, God then impressed upon Ezekiel the gravity of his call, emphasizing that this vocation was not merely a personal aspiration—an opportunity to grow as a prophet. *The call of the watchman is a matter of life and death.* If Ezekiel was disobedient, the blood of the wicked and of the wayward right-eous would be upon his hands. If Ezekiel was obedient, he would have done his duty, not only delivering his own soul, but giving opportunity for others to hear and repent at the word of the Lord. *His obedience and disobedience had direct missional consequences.*

These consequences are connected to the very heart of God. Let's consider again Ezekiel 33, which we looked at in the begin-ning of the book. God repeated to Ezekiel what He had said in 3:17–21. This second time, there were a few revisions. First, instead of the message being applied only to Ezekiel personally, God applied it broadly to anyone called as a watchman. This reveals that missional obedience was not just for Ezekiel, but it is for all of us called by God. Secondly, God inserted His passion for those who would hear the watchmen's message. He told Ezekiel, "Say to them: 'As I live,' says the Lord GOD, 'I have no pleasure in the death of the wicked, but that the wicked turn from his way and live. Turn, turn from your evil ways! For why should you die, O house of Israel?'" (33:11). God is not indifferent to the people to whom He calls us. The pleasure of His heart is to see people turn away from wickedness and death, and turn back to righteousness and life. The watchman obeys not simply to wash his own hands. He obeys because God's passion for people beats within the watchman's heart, and the watchman is not indifferent to their condition either.

Incarnational Prophets

If you look closely at Ezekiel's life, you'll see that his obedience was a combination of both words and actions. He was both vocal and incarnational with his message. Ezekiel *said* what God said, and he *embodied* what God said. The prophetic call of the watchman demands that we do both—speak and act upon the word of the Lord.

Throughout Scripture, prophets were preachers of God's word as well as physical signs of God's word. Isaiah captured this in Isaiah 8:18: "Here am I and the children whom the LORD has given me! We are for signs and wonders in Israel from the LORD of hosts, who dwells in Mount Zion." *Isaiah didn't just speak what God was saying. He and his family literally became what God was saying.* When Isaiah and his wife (which he refers to as "the prophetess") conceived and bore children, God gave them specific names, each one a message to Israel. Their *lives* were a physical sign of God's audible voice.

The prophet Hosea lived in a similar manner. God told Hosea to *talk* to Israel about her adulterous heart. Furthermore, God told Hosea to *live the story* and embody God's heart toward Israel through his own actions: "Then the LORD said to me, 'Go again, love a woman who is loved by a lover and is committing adultery, just like the love of the LORD for the children of Israel, who look to other gods and love the raisin cakes of the pagans'" (Hos. 3:1).

From this commandment, Hosea purchased and married a harlot. Then, from his obedience, the promise of God proceeded to Israel. Hosea's actions became a reference point for God's actions and then pointed toward God's ultimate redemptive faithfulness.

The prophet Zechariah also *acted* according to God's word, and his actions became an embodiment of prophecy:

> I took for myself two staffs: the one I called Beauty, and the other I called Bonds. . . . And I took my staff, Beauty, and cut it in two, that I might break the covenant which I had made with all the peoples. So it was broken on that day. Thus the poor of the flock, who were watching me, knew it was the word of the Lord. (Zechariah 11:7, 10–11)

When the flock *saw* what Zechariah did, they knew what God was *saying*.

Just like Isaiah, Hosea, and Zechariah, Ezekiel was no exception to being an incarnational prophet. God commanded Ezekiel to act in ways that spoke to the children of Israel. Then, as Ezekiel obeyed in his actions, God explained that his actions were signs, pointing to and revealing God's message. Furthermore, Ezekiel's actions were not just signs, but he himself was a sign. In Ezekiel 12:6, God told him, "I have made you a sign to the house of Israel." Then, God instructed him to explain this vocation to Israel: "Say [to the children of Israel], 'I am a sign to you'" (12:11). Later, God repeated this to Israel Himself: "Ezekiel is a sign to you" (24:24). The repetitive nature of this theme reveals its importance. Watchmen do not just declare what God says or privately obey what God says; *they* are a declaration from God. To be that, you must submit your life to the voice of God in unusual ways.

God told Ezekiel to do bizarre things. These bizarre instructions didn't wait until later in Ezekiel's prophetic ministry, once he was acclimated to the watchman lifestyle. Such instructions come early in the book of Ezekiel, following his initial call. It seems God wanted to establish early in the process that incarnational living was necessary to the watchman call. Ezekiel 4 is full of examples. First, God told Ezekiel to construct a model city and stage a siege. Then, he had to lay on his left side 390 days. Next, he had to lay on his right side 40 days. While on his side, God gave Ezekiel a strict diet. Ezekiel also had to prepare his meals in a certain way—by cooking them over human dung. When Ezekiel objected, God agreed to let him cook over cow dung instead. In the next chapter, Ezekiel was required to shave his head and beard with a sword and then burn his hair publicly. These bizarre actions introduced Ezekiel to his audience and set the stage for his messages. And the actions didn't stop after the early chapters of his book. As the book progresses, these bizarre happenings become much more personal for Ezekiel. When his wife died in chapter 24, God restricted Ezekiel from grieving in the customary way, though the prophet was deeply distressed by her death. This radical submission to the voice of God demonstrated the requirements for being a sign. You become a demonstration of God's word through obeying God's word, regardless of the cost.

Of course, all these examples in the Old Testament anticipate Jesus Christ Himself. As John 1:14 explains, "And the Word became flesh and dwelt among us." Jesus did not only speak God's word or act according to God's word. He was and is God's Word. He embodies the very essence of who God is, what God wants, and what God says, because, of course, He is God. This mystery is described in John 1:1: "In the beginning was the Word, and the Word was with God, and the Word was God." Jesus is the living, visible embodiment of the invisible God, as Paul, the apostle, wrote in Colossians 1:15: "He is the image of the invisible God." If the world wonders what God wants, what God says, and what God is like, they must look at Jesus to find the answers. In *The Knowledge of the Holy*, A. W. Tozer wrote, "Now someone . . . may cautiously inquire, 'If I come to God, how will He act toward me? What kind of disposition has He? What will I find Him to be like?' The answer is that He will be found to be exactly like

Jesus."[1] *Jesus is the Sign, but more than that, Jesus is the Message.* What's more, Jesus is not just the Message and the Messenger, but the One who sends the message. He is all.

Not all of this has an application for us because Jesus is unique in His identity and His glory. Yet there is a partial application for us because Christ dwells in us by the power of His Spirit, and we are predestined to be conformed to His image (see Rom. 8:9, 29). In no way are we called to be God, but we are called to demonstrate God. We are called, like Ezekiel, to be a sign to others. *We are called to live an incarnational life, and this is made possible for new covenant believers because of the power of Christ in our lives.* Colossians 1:27 describes this reality: "Christ in you, the hope of glory." As Christ lives in us and through us, we partake of His glory. An element of that glory is to manifest through a physical, living body the word, will, and nature of God.

It's this combination of hearing, praying, declaring, obeying, and embodying God's word that comprises missional obedience. Ezekiel modeled it. Jesus demonstrated it perfectly. And after Jesus, Paul gave us another reference point for this lifestyle.

We may not typically think of Paul as a watchman, but there are watchman characteristics to his life. To begin with, his conversion was a holy interruption. It may not have been a fiery whirlwind, but it was no less forceful. After Ezekiel's God-encounter, he sat by the River Chebar, astonished and speechless for seven days. After Paul's God-encounter, he was "astonished" and sat "three days without sight, and neither ate nor drank" (Acts 9:6, 9). Like Ezekiel's experience, this moment was not a mere addition to Paul's life, but a radical interruption that brought him into orbit around the amber heart of God. Also, Paul cultivated prophetic sensitivity. His articulation of the gospel did not come from scholarship, but from revelation: "But I make known to you, brethren, that the gospel which was preached by me is not according to man. For I neither received it from man, nor was I taught it, but it came through the revelation of Jesus Christ" (Gal. 1:11–12). Like the watchmen, it's the revelatory realm that initiated and fueled his ministry. What's more is this gospel compelled Paul's intercessory posture. He frequently described his prayer life on behalf of the churches, writing things like, "My little children, for whom I labor in birth again until Christ is formed in you . . ." (Gal. 4:19). With prophetic sensitivity and an intercessory heart, Paul lived in missional obedience.

Paul's missional obedience was first described to him by Jesus Himself. Recounting his conversion in Acts 26:15–16, Paul explained that Jesus said to him: "I am Jesus, whom you are persecuting. But rise and stand on your feet; for I have appeared to you for this purpose, to make you a minister and a witness both of the things which you have seen and of the things which I will yet reveal to you." Paul would not just speak and write about the things he saw. He was not only a witness to them; Jesus first said he would be a "minister" of those things. According to *Strong's*, the Greek word is literally "an under-oarsman."[2] The image is that of someone in the galley of a ship, rowing to move the ship forward. What Paul saw, Paul must first embody through obedience and hard work, humbly moving forward into the call of God. Jesus also referred to Paul's incarnational call when He instructed Ananias to pray for Paul in Acts 9:15: "But the Lord said to him, 'Go, for he is a chosen vessel of Mine to bear My name before Gentiles, kings, and the children of Israel.'" Paul didn't simply declare the name of Jesus. He *bore* the name of Jesus. He carried it. He embodied it. Like it did for Ezekiel, this required sacrificial obedience. In the next verse, Jesus described this, saying, "For I will show him how many things he must suffer for My name's sake" (9:16). Paul's missional obedience included suffering for the name he carried. Then, from this sacrificial, incarnational demonstration of God's word, Paul would vocalize God's message.

Words Matter

I'm emphasizing the action side of obedience, but I also want to make sure we value and embrace the *vocal* side of obedience. While Jesus did say to Paul that Paul would be a "minister," He also said Paul would be a "witness." That meant describing what he saw with words. While Jesus called Paul to do more than speak and write, He did not call him to do less. The watchman must not only see and act, but also *declare* what he sees. An important aspect to prophetic sensitivity is disciplined silenced, but the call of the prophet doesn't end there. *Prophetic sensitivity leads to prophetic responsibility, which includes both intercession and public declaration.* God shut Ezekiel's mouth in order for Ezekiel to hear, but then He opened Ezekiel's mouth in order for Ezekiel to speak: "But when I speak with you, I will open your mouth" (Ezek. 3:27). *The eyes, ears, and heart of the watchman find expression through his or her mouth.* As much as God told Ezekiel to watch, He also told him to declare. This is captured clearly in Ezekiel 40:4: "Declare to the house of Israel everything you see." For both Ezekiel and Paul, access to revelation compelled them to speak.

Actions do not fully translate into a message until we articulate them in speech. God would tell Ezekiel to act in bizarre ways and then give Ezekiel the interpretation of his actions. Without the interpretation, the actions would only provoke curiosity, but not deliver a message. *The two need to work together: actions provoking questions and speech giving answers.* In Ezekiel 37, God instructed Ezekiel to unite two sticks into one. He then said, "And when the children of your people speak to you, saying, 'Will you not show us what you mean by these?'—say to them . . ." (37:18–19). Ezekiel's obedience created an opportunity to say something in a way that pierced their hearts. The same thing happened when his wife died. When Ezekiel didn't mourn for her, it led to a question: "And the people said to me, 'Will you not tell us what these things signify to us, that you behave so?'" (24:19). The action provoked a question to which the word of the Lord was the answer. The action was important, but Ezekiel's words articulated the message.

Words matter. What you say and what you write have a profound impact on the world around you. In a materialistic, pragmatic culture, we sometimes believe that only actions and widgets matter. We prioritize the things we can touch, hold, and count. According to Scripture, the material, visible realm comes from the invisible, vocal realm. God *spoke* creation into existence. Hebrews 11:3 says, "By faith we understand that the worlds were framed by the word of God, so that things which are seen were not made of things which are visible." Our world was framed by God's *word*. What God said gave our world existence, definition, and meaning. Furthermore, that reality is not just an origination issue, something that was necessary in the past. It is a present issue, a current reality. Hebrews 1:3 describes Jesus as presently, right now "upholding all things by the word of His power." His word continues to sustain creation.

When we understand the power of words, it gives us great sobriety about what we say and the fact that we ought to be speaking. It gives us the dual conviction of disciplined silence to hear and prophetic responsibility to speak. The New Testament apostles modeled this dual call. In Acts 6, turmoil arose in the church because there was a practical need among the Hellenist widows. When faced with this dilemma, the apostles did not minimize the legitimacy of the need, but neither did they detract from their primary role within the church. They delegated the issue to capable leaders, and then they focused on their vocation, saying, "We will give ourselves continually to prayer and to the ministry of the word" (6:4). In this verse, we see two important components of the watchman lifestyle: (1) prayer, where the heart can stay in rhythm with God, hear the Lord's counsel, and respond through intercessory love; and (2) the ministry of the word, where the mouth can deliver publicly what God is saying to shape the community and lead people to righteousness. Like Ezekiel, from the secluded place of prayerful listening, the apostles would emerge with the word of the Lord for the people of God.

Our words matter, and our actions matter. Understanding this leads to missional obedience, knowing that our lives have real consequence. Obedience is not just an issue of private accountability to God. Obedience creates opportunity for others to hear, see, and believe in God. It opens the door for others to escape death and find eternal life in Jesus Christ.

PART THREE
WHAT TO WATCH

CHAPTER NINE

THE COUNSEL OF THE LORD

So far, I've been describing a lot of the watchman's internal world: prophetic sensitivity, intercessory love, and missional obedience, all built upon friendship with God. But what about the watchman's external world? If a watchman is called to watch, what he is watching for? What is he looking for as his eyes are open, gazing across the horizon?

Though the answer to these questions could be quite vast, I want to explore six areas with you over the next several chapters. Each of these areas have a theme and a corresponding question that will help us activate our eyes in the discipline of watching. We will discuss the first question in this chapter and each of the other questions in the next five chapters. Here is what we'll cover:

1. The counsel of the Lord: What is God saying?
2. The condition of your soul: How am I doing?
3. The condition of our community: How are we doing?
4. The strategies of the enemy: What is Satan attempting?
5. The answers to our prayers: Where is God moving?
6. The return of the Lord: How am I preparing?

What Is God Saying?

We must begin with the counsel of the Lord, asking, what is God saying? This area shouldn't come as a surprise. In many ways, I've covered it already, describing the responsibility of the watchman to cultivate prophetic sensitivity. You sharpen your prophetic senses through biblical literacy and disciplined silence. Additionally, it is the counsel of the Lord that initiates effective intercession. Abraham contended for Sodom because God revealed to him God's secret counsel, asking, "Shall I hide from Abraham what I am doing. . . ?" (Gen. 18:17). Because God didn't hide His plans from Abraham, Abraham became a watchman for the city and for his nephew, Lot.

Though I've covered this topic already, I want to revisit it because, as watchmen, we can never stray from this fundamental call. As we watch, it is tempting to judge circumstances based upon what we see in the natural realm. If we do that, though, we live reactionarily. Remember that reactionary watchmen are not truly watchmen, but merely social commentators. They may inform others about what is happening, but they don't leverage spiritual authority to create change. We must discern the natural realm by interpreting it from the spiritual realm. *The counsel of the Lord gives us authority in prayer and weight when we speak.* It clarifies our minds to think properly about what we see in the world around us, and, thus, it equips us to respond with God's heart. It is essential to ask, "What is God saying?" He doesn't despise us for asking that question. In fact, God loves inquisitive hearts.

Inquisitive Hearts

King David had a special relationship with God. First Samuel 13:14 describes him in this way: "The LORD has sought for

Himself a man after His own heart." As a man after God's own heart, David was not a perfect man, but he possessed qualities that God values, many of which were captured in the Psalms. In Psalm 27:4, David described the driving motive of his life: "One thing I have desired of the LORD, that will I seek: that I may dwell in the house of the LORD all the days of my life, to behold the beauty of the LORD, and to inquire in His temple." David described his driving motive as "one thing," but he then expressed it in three ways. He wanted to "dwell," "behold," and "inquire." How do you reconcile the "one thing" statement with the three-things description? David was describing three facets of one thing. His one thing was an insatiable hunger for God. That one hunger expressed itself in three ways: a desire to be with God (dwell), to see God (behold), and to know God (inquire). David wanted access to God's presence, revelation, and counsel. The counsel of the Lord is an inseparable part of seeking Him. David desired to have it, and that desire moved God's heart.

In 2 Samuel 5:17–25, we find an example of how David lived dependent upon the Lord's counsel. Shortly after David became king of all Israel, the Philistines attacked. You would assume David's confidence level was at an all-time high and that he was itching to lead Israel's army to victory as king. After all, he had defeated the Philistine champion, Goliath, as a youth, causing Israel to rout the remaining Philistines from the battlefield. If that was what the boy David did, surely then those old enemies would be no challenge for the newly anointed king. However, David's first response was not to muster the troops and deliver a battle plan. His first response was to inquire of the Lord: "The Philistines also went and deployed themselves in the Valley of Rephaim. So David inquired of the LORD, saying, 'Shall I go up against the Philistines? Will You deliver them into my hand?" (2 Sam. 5:18–19). Because he paused and inquired, the Lord answered him. The ensuing victory was so significant that David described it like this: "The LORD has broken through my enemies before me, like the breakthrough of water" (2 Sam. 5:20). The Lord broke through on David's behalf because David first asked the Lord for His counsel.

Next, the Philistines tried their luck again and staged another attack. Surely, this time David was confident enough to act on his own. As a boy, he saw victory, and as king, he had seen victory. But David refused to put his trust in himself. Again, he paused and inquired: "Then the Philistines went up once again and deployed themselves in the Valley of Rephaim. Therefore David inquired of the LORD" (2 Sam. 5:22–23). David saw victory once more through obeying the Lord's instruction. This second pause to inquire impresses me more than the first one. I expected David to ask the Lord for counsel in his first battle as king, but I didn't expect him to ask a second time, right on the heels of a stunning victory. This second, unexpected inquiry reveals a lot about David. He wasn't just concerned about the result of the battle. *David wanted to make sure he stayed in rhythm with God. He wanted to lead from a place of friendship and fellowship with the God who called him to be king in the first place.*

The desire to inquire was a distinguishing mark of David. It was one of the differences between him and his predecessor, Saul. First Chronicles 10:13–14 gives interesting commentary on Saul's life, death, and transition of authority to David:

> So Saul died for his unfaithfulness which he had committed against the LORD, because he did not keep the word of the LORD, and also because he consulted a medium for guidance. But he did not inquire of the LORD; therefore He killed him, and turned the kingdom over to David the Son of Jesse.

According to these verses, Saul's failure to inquire was one of the key reasons he died and his house lost the throne. Rather than consulting the Lord, he consulted a medium. That story is found in 1 Samuel 28:3–25. What's interesting about that account is what it says about Saul just before he consulted the medium: "And when Saul inquired of the LORD, the LORD did not answer him, either by dreams or by Urim or by the prophets" (1 Sam. 28:6). In this verse, it clearly says that Saul "inquired of the LORD," but 1 Chronicles says that Saul "did not inquire of the LORD." How do we reconcile this contradiction?

When David described his desire to inquire, it was within the context of pursuit. David didn't inquire of the Lord merely in moments of crisis. He didn't use God like an encyclopedia or search engine, tossing questions to God when he didn't know what to do. David inquired as an expression of his hunger for God in every area of his life. It's the third facet of his "one thing" lifestyle. Before he asked God questions, David first wanted to be with Him (dwell) and to see Him (behold). Saul, on the other hand, did not inquire as an expression of hunger for God. He didn't seem interested in the friendship and fellowship David pursued. Saul simply wanted answers to questions and solutions to problems. Thus, when he didn't get them from God in an expedient timeframe, he quickly turned to other sources. Saul may have technically inquired of the Lord, but it wasn't the Psalm 27:4 inquiry of the Lord that God was looking for. This was evident in Saul's unwillingness to wait.

This is really important for the lifestyle of the watchman. *When we ask God questions, it needs to come from the overflow of our pursuit of Him.* We can't treat the counsel of the Lord like a spiritual news program, giving us updates to satisfy our curiosity. We must inquire of Him because we want to be in rhythm with Him. We must inquire of Him because we want our lives to revolve around His amber heart.

When David used the word *inquire,* it contained much more than we realize. The website www.blueletterbible.org breaks down the different senses in which *inquire* is used in Scripture:

1. To resort to, frequent, (tread a place)
2. To consult, enquire of, seek God
3. To seek [God] in prayer and worship
4. To seek (with a demand), demand, require

5. To investigate
6. To ask for, require, demand
7. To practice, study, follow, seek with application
8. To seek with care[1]

I like meditating on each of these because they reveal how robust the activity of inquiring really is. It's not just asking occasional questions, but frequently pursuing God. The pursuit includes "prayer and worship." Your heart "investigates" the nature of God, the Word of God, and the will of God. You do this not just for information's sake, but because you intend to "practice" and apply what you find. You "seek with care" as you pursue the Lord. Saul may have asked for God's advice, but he did not truly inquire of the Lord. David was different. Because he inquired, he moved God's heart.

Another person in Scripture with a unique relationship with God is David's son Solomon. Second Samuel 12:24–25 describes God's heart toward Solomon at his birth:

> Then David comforted Bathsheba his wife, and went in to her and lay with her. So she bore a son, and he called his name Solomon. Now the LORD loved him, and He sent word by the hand of Nathan the prophet: So he called his name Jedidiah, because of the LORD.

The second name of Solomon, Jedidiah, means, "Beloved of the LORD."[2] God had a special love for Solomon that wasn't explained further in this passage, but later scriptures give insight into Solomon's heart toward God. Like David, Solomon was by no means perfect. By the end of his life, he strayed quite seriously from God, engaging in idolatry and leading the nation into sin. Yet, early in his reign, we see a glimpse into the heart relationship between God and Solomon.

After Solomon offered sacrifices to God at Gibeon, God visited him in a dream: "At Gibeon the LORD appeared to Solomon in a dream by night; and God said, 'Ask! What shall I give you?'" (1 Kings 3:5). Solomon responded, "'Give to Your servant an understanding heart to judge Your people, that I may discern between good and evil. For who is able to judge this great people of Yours?'" (3:9). When Solomon asked for an "understanding heart," the literal translation is a "hearing heart."[3] He knew that true discernment came from God's counsel—not from Solomon's own ability to assess a situation. Solomon needed to hear what God was saying. It's often said that Solomon asked God for wisdom, but that is not entirely accurate. Solomon didn't ask for a wisdom that was disconnected from God. He wanted the ability to perceive the world through God's perspective. He wanted God's voice to direct his judgments. That, of course, is the essence of wisdom, but it is a wisdom dependent upon God. This desire from Solomon touched God's heart: "The speech pleased the Lord, that Solomon had asked this thing" (3:10). Perhaps, this quality of Solomon was what God anticipated at his birth, calling him, "Jedidiah."

When we read James in the New Testament, it ought to call this Solomon episode to mind. James wrote, "If any of you lacks wisdom, let him ask of God, who gives to all liberally and without reproach, and it will be given to him" (1:5). When we ask God for wisdom, for counsel, He doesn't reproach us for that. He doesn't roll His eyes because we don't know what to do. In fact, just the opposite is true. Like Solomon, it pleases the Lord when we ask. Like David, it reveals that we are after His heart and not our own way or agenda.

"As I Hear, I Judge"

Jesus perfectly models this Spirit-counsel lifestyle. Prophesying about Him as the Messiah, Isaiah 11:3 said, "He shall not judge by the sight of His eyes, nor decide by the hearing of His ears." The nations look expectantly to the judgments of Jesus because they're not rooted in the mere physical "sight of His eyes" or "hearing of His ears." His judgments come from a higher plane of information. Not only does the world long for this kind of judge, but God the Father is looking for this, too. *God entrusts Jesus with all judgment because He knows that Jesus will use His authority to implement only what He hears from the Father.* In John 5:22, Jesus affirmed how much the Father trusts Him, saying, "For the Father judges no one, but has committed all judgment to the Son." This is quite a high honor. The Father has delegated to His Son all judgment regarding humanity. Later in the chapter, Jesus also explained *why* the Father has this kind of trust in Him: "I can of Myself do nothing. As I hear, I judge; and My judgment is righteous, because I do not seek My own will but the will of the Father who sent Me" (John 5:30). *The Father perfectly trusts the Son because the Son is perfectly dependent upon the Father.* Jesus doesn't rely upon His own senses to judge. He relies upon His Father's counsel.

Left to our own understanding, we will not see the world properly. We need the Spirit to guide us. Paul captured this reality in 1 Corinthians. He explained, "But he who is spiritual judges all things, yet he himself is rightly judged by no one" (2:15). *It is the spiritual person, the spiritually guided person, the spiritually attuned person that "judges all things," discerning them properly and seeing them accurately.* That person is in rhythm with God, though his words and actions are misunderstood by others, though "he himself is rightly judged by no one." In the prior verse, Paul explained why the misunderstanding occurs: "But the natural man does not receive the things of the Spirit of God, for they are foolishness to him; nor can he know them, because they are spiritually discerned" (2:14). The "natural man" is not just a description of non-Christians, but of those who are thinking with mere human thinking. Naturally minded people—both non-Christians and Christians—cannot access the counsel of God until they step into spiritual discernment. Of course, the first step for unbelievers is to put their faith in Jesus.

Jesus said, "Most assuredly, I say to you, unless one is born again, he cannot see the kingdom of God" (John 3:3). Being born again opens our eyes to see. Then, the call for Christians is to grow in spiritual maturity. That's why Paul wrote, "However, we speak wisdom among those who are mature" (1 Cor. 2:6). *Maturity is not about age; it is about sensitivity to the Spirit.* Like Jesus, maturity for the believer is utter dependence upon the Father to equip our eyes with His lenses. This way of seeing, discerning, and judging the world is what I refer to as *the counsel of the Lord.*

To access the counsel of the Lord, we must ask, "What is God saying?" It's not enough to know what is happening in the world around us. We need to know what God is saying about it. Furthermore, what God is saying may or may not be a direct response to current events featured in the news. There are times when the topics on His mind may not be the topics on our minds. What's important to Him may not be the thing driving TV ratings or social media trends. That's why the first question to ask as a watchman is, "God, what are You saying?" We begin with His counsel first, not second. The progression is not, "Here is what's happening in the world. God, what are You saying about it?" The progression begins with His counsel and then goes from there.

A friend of mine named Shiloh had a dream that demonstrates this point well. In the dream, she was reading the book *Rees Howells: Intercessor* by Norman Grubb. She was in the room with her father and wanted to talk to him about the book. Every time she brought it up, though, he responded with one word, saying, "Israel." She was surprised each time and wanted to redirect the conversation. However, her father persisted in his one-word response: "Israel." After waking up from the dream, she knew what it meant. In the context of intercession, Israel was on the Father's mind. Though she wanted to talk about other things, He wanted to talk about that.

How often do we, like Shiloh, come to God with a predetermined conversation in mind? Are we willing to quiet our souls long enough to hear what may be on the heart of God? One of my favorite verses regarding prayer is found in Ecclesiastes 5:1–2:

> Walk prudently when you go to the house of God; and draw near to hear rather than to give the sacrifice of fools, for they do not know that they do evil. Do not be rash with your mouth, and let not your heart utter anything hastily before God. For God is in heaven, and you on earth; therefore let your words be few.

These verses have different layers of application. One application is about the starting point of prayer. They admonish to "draw near to hear." How often do we draw near to speak without first drawing near to hear? How often do we only unburden our hearts without asking God about His heart? *If we would slow down and ask the Lord for His counsel, it would change the dynamics of our prayers.*

As I wrote earlier, the most effective intercession flows from the initiatives of God. First John 5:14–15 explains, "Now this is the confidence that we have in Him, that if we ask anything according to His will, He hears us. And if we know that He hears us, whatever we ask, we know that we have the petitions that we have asked of Him." These two verses teach us how to have "confidence" in prayer. Having confidence in prayer begins with the Lord's counsel. Asking "according to His will" produces results. *Effective intercession is a partnership with God concerning the desires of God.*

Rather than paralyzing our prayers, this reality ought to energize us in prayer. God loves inquisitive hearts. He doesn't resent us for having to ask Him, "What are You saying?" or "What is on Your heart?" Those questions move Him deeply, and He responds to them.

CHAPTER TEN

THE CONDITION OF YOUR SOUL

ONCE WE ASK THE LORD WHAT HE IS SAYING, WE THEN NEED TO ASK, *"How am I doing?"* We need to use His counsel to assess our own spiritual health. The call for the watchman is not to hear from God and then immediately apply what He says to everyone else. The call is to hear from God and let that truth become a personal, transformational reality. *First, the counsel of the Lord speaks to our internal condition, and, second, it speaks through us to the world.*

This is a part of missional obedience. As Jesus told Paul, we are to be both ministers and witnesses of the things God shows us. We can't be proper witnesses if we skip the step of being ministers. In that step, God's Word goes deep into our inner world and finds traction through our lifestyle. Remember, the word for *minister* in Acts 26:16 is *under oarsmen.* Below the surface, a minister works in the belly of the ship, moving it forward in the sea. In the same way, the Lord's counsel must go beyond the surface of a ministry persona. It must get into our bellies and shape our movements, our actions, our lives. That's why God not only told Ezekiel to eat, but He also told him, "Son of man, feed your belly, and fill your stomach with this scroll that I give you" (3:3). He didn't want Ezekiel to merely taste the scroll. God wanted it to reach Ezekiel's belly and fill his stomach. God wanted Ezekiel to digest His word until it became an inseparable part of his being.

We watch not only for cities and nations, but also for our own souls. If we don't, we'll be vulnerable to spiritual deterioration. *Even if we have a reputation for spiritual health, the reality of our condition may be otherwise.* When Jesus addresses the church in Sardis, He identifies a threat we all face: "I know your works, that you have a name that you are alive, but you are dead" (Rev. 3:1). Through our works toward others, it's possible to establish a name that people respect. However, behind the visage of spirituality, Jesus sees the reality. This is why we need the counsel of the Lord. Without it, we tend to deceive ourselves *and* others about how we are doing. Understanding this reality, David wrote, "Who can understand his errors? Cleanse me from secret faults. Keep back your servant also from presumptuous sins; let them not have dominion over me. Then I shall be blameless, and I shall be innocent of great transgression" (Ps. 19:12–13). When we don't invite the Lord's counsel into our lives, we are riddled with "secret faults." Our own "errors" have "dominion" over us, ruling our lives. We commit "presumptuous sins" because we are unaware of them, allowing self-assured pride to create blind spots. We need God to open our eyes to our condition.

We need to watch for our own souls. In fact, this is the solution Jesus gives to Sardis. After He describes their condition, He tells them, "Be watchful" (Rev. 3:2). This implies two things. First, the reason they are spiritually dead is because they failed to watch. Had they been watching, they wouldn't have spiraled into such a state of decline. Secondly, if they do watch, they can correct course and move in a different direction. *Restoring the watchmen will restore the life of the Church—as long as what they see is applied personally to them and not just to others through them.*

Examine Yourself

Our internal world is a dynamic place that we must constantly monitor. It is not static. It is always going somewhere as it processes fluctuating ideas, emotions, and circumstances. Left to itself, there's no telling where it might go. We must, therefore, guide it and assess it by the Word of the Lord. In 2 Corinthians 13:5, Paul charged, "Examine yourselves as to whether you are in the faith. Test yourselves." His words call us to healthy introspection. If we don't "test" and "examine" ourselves, we may not be where we think we are. Like the church in Sardis, we may think we are alive when we are dead. We may think we are "in the faith" when we're no longer living by faith. The results can be disastrous.

In 1 Corinthians 11:27–31, Paul applied this charge to the communion table:

> Therefore whoever eats this bread or drinks this cup of the Lord in an unworthy manner will be guilty of the body and blood of the Lord. But let a man examine himself, and so let him eat of the bread and drink of the cup. For he who eats and drinks in an unworthy manner eats and drinks judgment to himself, not discerning the Lord's body. For this reason many are weak and sick among you, and many sleep. For if we would judge ourselves, we would not be judged.

According to Paul, "many are weak and sick" within the Church because they are failing to examine themselves. They are not judging themselves, assessing their spiritual condition. "Many sleep" because they absentmindedly receive communion without pausing to consider their true spiritual state. This passage reveals how dangerous it is to go through religious motions without truly watching for our souls. *The dynamic inner world will move into unhealthy places unless the counsel of the Lord bridles it.*

Paul not only charged the Church with this principle, but he also lived it himself. In 1 Corinthians 9:27, he wrote, "But I discipline my body and bring it into subjection, lest, when I have preached to others, I myself should become disqualified." He knew that merely carrying a message didn't guarantee his internal, spiritual health. Rather, it made him more vulnerable. Therefore, he examined, judged, and disciplined himself. Without that kind of intentionality, his life would have veered off course, leaving him disqualified.

Those who have influence among others are in a peculiar place of vulnerability. When God speaks or works through you, you must actively remind yourself that you are not better than those to whom you minister. Especially when the work of God through you involves confronting sin, it can make you overlook your own propensity toward sin. However, *you are human and vulnerable to the same temptations God is using you to confront.* Paul described this in Galatians 6:1–5:

> Brethren, if a man is overtaken in any trespass, you who are spiritual restore such a one in a spirit of gentleness, considering yourself lest you also be tempted. Bear one another's burdens, and so fulfill the law of Christ. For if anyone thinks himself to be something, when he is nothing, he deceives himself. But let each one examine his own work, and then he will have rejoicing in himself alone, and not in another. For each one shall bear his own load.

In this passage, Paul gave prerequisites and guidelines for dealing with a brother who is "overtaken" with "trespass." These instructions create the healthiest environment for both the one who is being restored and the one who is restoring. Before engaging, you must be "spiritual." It can't be your impatience with people that drives you to confront their issues. We must be spiritually motivated and animated by love. Otherwise, like Ezekiel, our mouths should be shut, and our tongues should cling to the roof of our mouths. This spiritual starting point leads to engaging with "a spirit of gentleness." If we are not gentle and kind, we're not operating in love. There is a way to be direct and intense with your message while still delivering it in a spirit of gentleness. *As watch-*

men, it's important to remember that the end goal of confrontation is restoration. We don't confront for the sake of confrontation. After Paul identified the prerequisite of a "spiritual" person with a "spirit of gentleness," he then added this warning: "considering yourself lest you also be tempted." While engaging with others, we can't neglect ourselves. We can't forget that our own souls need watching, tending, and protecting. If we neglect ourselves, we could fall into temptation.

This self-awareness is a mark of humility. In his book *A Treatise on Prayer*, Edward Bickersteth recounted the story of John Bradford, whose famous statement demonstrated the kind of humble self-awareness and personal consideration each of us must possess. He wrote,

> Those who know their own hearts will be ready to acknowledge that the seeds of the worst and most aggravated wickedness which have been practiced by other men lie hid therein . . . and are only restrained from bursting forth by God's grace. The pious Martyr Bradford, when he saw a poor criminal led to execution, exclaimed, "There, but for the grace of God, goes John Bradford." He knew that the same evil principles were in his own heart which had brought the criminal to that shameful end.[1]

As we look upon others who are "overtaken" by their sin, we need to see ourselves. We need to see a brother or sister with the same humanity we possess. Rather than looking with eyes of judgment or self-assurance, we must say, like Bradford, "There, but for the grace of God, go I." It is with this spirit that Paul wrote, "For if anyone thinks himself to be something, when he is nothing, he deceives himself." *When we think of ourselves as something beyond the reach of temptation, we make ourselves vulnerable to it. When we see ourselves as impenetrable, we create chinks the enemy can exploit.* This doesn't mean we should sin to keep ourselves humble. It means that we remain aware of the fragility and vulnerability of our own hearts. As Bickersteth writes, we "acknowledge that the seeds of . . . wickedness . . . are only restrained from bursting forth by God's grace." Therefore, while helping others, each one must "examine his own work." We must ask God and ourselves, "How am I doing?"

Proverbs 4:23 says, "Keep your heart with all diligence, for out of it spring the issues of life." Though it's not *šāmar*, the Hebrew word for *keep* here is occasionally translated in Scripture as "watchmen" or "watchers."[2] Your heart needs to be watched. It needs your spiritual senses awake to God. All the "issues of life" flow from the posture of your heart. Therefore, its incumbent upon you to watch, not only on the walls of your city and nation, but also upon the walls of your own life.

CHAPTER ELEVEN

THE CONDITION OF OUR COMMUNITY

THE WATCHMAN CALL HAS A DISTINCT COMMUNITY ELEMENT. THOUGH it begins as an individual interaction between God and the watchman, its primary vocation is communal. *God raises up watchmen because He loves human communities, and He wants to protect them through the vision, prayer, and message of the watchmen.* Thus, as we hear God's counsel, we may begin with, "How am I doing?" but it must quickly become, "How are *we* doing?"

When I use the word *community,* I mean it in a variety of ways. Broadly, I mean the nations and cities to which God assigns us. I also use it to describe any kind of community to which God has connected you. This includes your church congregation, friend group, family, and marriage. A community is any sphere that extends beyond yourself and includes someone else in a meaningful relationship. Within these spheres, we have a responsibility to live the watchman lifestyle of prophetic sensitivity, intercessory love, and missional obedience.

In Hebrews 13:17, Scripture describes the watchman role that leaders have within congregations: "Obey those who rule over you, and be submissive, for they watch out for your souls, as those who must give account." *Leaders within the Body of Christ are not simply speakers, counselors, or administrators. They are watchmen.* Their ministry consists of living in rhythm with God, staying aware of both His counsel and the Church's condition. Their leadership maneuvers between the two. As they look at the Church's condition through the lens of God's Word, they guide the Church away from dangers into the abundance and health of God's promises.

Though there is a specific role for leaders to be watchmen, they are not the only ones responsible. Each of us has a responsibility toward our brothers and sisters in the Lord. In Genesis 4, we find the story of Cain and Abel. It's a tragic story where Cain's envy drove him to murder his own brother. Notice how Cain responded when God confronted him: "Then the LORD said to Cain, 'Where is Abel your brother?' He said, 'I do not know. Am I my brother's keeper?'" (Gen. 4:9) The Hebrew word for *keeper* is *šāmar*, the same word translated "watchman" in Isaiah 62. Thus, Cain asked God, "Am I my brother's watchman?" The answer is, "Yes, you are, Cain"; otherwise, God wouldn't have asked him the question. If God asked us, "Where is your brother? Where is your sister?" would we know what to say? Would we know how to respond? Or are we so obsessed with our own issues that we don't see beyond ourselves?

You see, *as we become our own watchman, it equips us to be a watchman for others.* When you consistently ask, "How am I doing?" it prepares you to ask, "How are we doing?" It's a bit counterintuitive, but it's true. Cain couldn't properly be Abel's watchman because he wasn't his own watchman first. Before Cain murdered Abel, God warned him, "[S]in lies at the door. And its desire is for you, but you should rule over it" (Gen. 4:7). God warned Cain that sin was just outside the door of his heart, ready to invade, ready to pounce! Cain refused to see it or refused to care. The end result was blinding rage, destroying both him and his brother. Guarding your heart is an act of love, not only for yourself, but also for your community. *When you personally submit*

to the Lord's counsel, it prepares you to see the condition of others. And
when you see their condition through eyes of love, it leads to intercession
that protects and supports them.

Intercessors or Accusers?

Jesus modeled how to be a watchman for those around us. In
Luke 22, He prophetically saw Satan mounting an attack on Peter:
"And the Lord said, 'Simon, Simon! Indeed, Satan has asked for
you, that he may sift you as wheat'" (v. 31). Jesus saw the attack
coming, and He knew Peter was vulnerable. What did He do with
the information? He prayed: "But I have prayed for you, that your
faith should not fail" (22:32). Jesus was not disinterested or indifferent to what Peter was about to face. His prophetic sensitivity
drove Him to intercessory love. Furthermore, Jesus spoke words
of destiny that carried Peter beyond the attack: "And when you
have returned to Me, strengthen your brethren" (v. 32). Jesus
knew Peter would succumb to temptation, but He looked beyond
that to his prophetic destiny and identity. Jesus interceded for him
based upon that reality.

Do we handle our brothers and sisters in this way? Are we
spiritually aware enough to sense when someone around us is
facing testing, trial, or attack? And if we do sense that, how do we
respond? Do we engage in intercession? Or do we smugly anticipate their failure? Furthermore, do we encourage them with
prophetic destiny beyond the trial?

In his classic devotional *My Utmost for His Highest*, Oswald
Chambers described how God will give you discernment
regarding someone else's spiritual condition to empower you as
an intercessor. He explained, "God gives us discernment in the
lives of others to call us to intercession for them, never so that we
may find fault with them."[1] Chambers reminds us that, if we

don't keep this call of intercession active, then we'll turn discernment into criticism:

> If we are not heedful and pay no attention to the way the Spirit of God works in us, we will become spiritual hypocrites. We see where other people are failing, and then we take our discernment and turn it into comments of ridicule and criticism, instead of turning it into intercession on their behalf. . . . One of the most subtle and illusive burdens God ever places on us as saints is this burden of discernment concerning others. He gives us discernment so that we may accept the responsibility for those souls before Him and form the mind of Christ about them.[2]

When we see someone else struggling, we have a choice to make. Like Jesus, we can become intercessors. Or, like Satan, we can become accusers. Watchmen choose the former, knowing it is their duty to guard the community God has given to them.

Wield the Sword of the Spirit

To see God's will manifested in our communities, we must take our place as watchmen. Otherwise, the community will be vulnerable to the enemy. In the garden of Eden, the fall of mankind was due in part to the neglect of the original watchman, Adam. Genesis 2:15 describes God's intention for Adam: "Then the LORD God took the man and put him in the garden of Eden to tend and keep it." His responsibility was not only to "tend" or cultivate the garden, but also to "keep it." The Hebrew word for *keep* is one we've already studied—*šāmar*. It's the same word Cain used in Genesis 4:9 and the word for *watchman* in Isaiah 62. God appointed Adam to be the watchman of Eden. Part of that role was to guard it, making sure what was in the garden was what was supposed to be there. We know this is an aspect of the watchman's role because of the way *šāmar* is used next.

After God sent Adam and Eve out of the garden, He stationed cherubim "to guard the way to the tree of life" (3:24). The word for *guard* is *šāmar*. The cherubim were the watchmen of the tree of life, restricting access to it. This gives us a reference point for Adam's role in Eden. He should have been governing its access points, remaining aware of anything that was contrary to God's design. The serpent questioning Eve about God's commandments should have set off warning sirens to Adam. At that moment, his watchman call should have activated. But Adam was silent while the serpent was talking. It is likely that Adam heard the conversation between Eve and the serpent because, after Eve ate the fruit, Scripture says, "She also gave to her husband with her" (3:6). Adam was *with her*. Though he was there, he was not keeping the garden and his wife as a watchman. Conversely, the tree of life cherubim modeled what Adam should have done. These creatures wielded a "flaming sword which turned every way" (3:24). The New Testament identifies "the sword of the Spirit" as "the word of God" (Eph. 6:17). Seen in that context, the cherubim wielded the fiery Word of God to protect the tree of life. That Word turned "every way," guarded every access point, answered every question, and settled every debate. Adam could have protected Eve had he, like the cherubim, used God's Word to silence the serpent.

God doesn't want us to simply be *in* community. He wants us to be watchmen *for* our community. It's wonderful that we are with people. *Yet we also need to be an active presence of intercession for the people we are with, using the Word of God to dispel the lies of the enemy.* Otherwise, those lies will have unrestricted, unchallenged access to our cities, churches, friends, and families. In Ephesians 6, after Paul listed the weapons of our spiritual warfare, he then charged the believers with how to use them: "praying always with all prayer and supplication in the Spirit, *being watchful* to this end with all perseverance and supplication for all the saints"

(6:18). In Paul's vision, spiritual warfare is not just an individual battle. It is a communal battle, and we all have a watchman role to pray on behalf of each other. With the sword of the Spirit, we engage in "all prayer and supplication . . . for all the saints."

This vision of communal spiritual warfare leads us to the next area of watching.

CHAPTER TWELVE

THE STRATEGIES OF THE ENEMY

As watchmen, we must be aware of the strategies of the enemy. We need to ask, *"What is Satan attempting to do?"* When Paul referred to spiritual warfare, he described it as standing against the "wiles of the devil" (Eph. 6:11). We cannot resist Satan's schemes if we don't know what they are. Our ignorance will leave us vulnerable. With awareness, however, we're able to defend our hearts appropriately, "lest Satan should take advantage of us; for we are not ignorant of his devices" (2 Cor. 2:11). When you know how the enemy works, you can minimize his ability to "take advantage" of you.

Even though this is an important part of the watchman's vigilance, I intentionally put it further down the list. Sometimes, it's tempting to place it as number one. When people hear about the watchman call, they can turn paranoid spiritually and obsess about potential demonic attacks. Suddenly, they attempt to track every movement of the enemy, highlighting to everyone what he is doing within communities. The problem with that approach, though, is that I don't see it in Scripture. Certainly, Scripture supports our having an awareness of the enemy (which I will describe later), but the prophets put the bulk of their focus on other areas. They emphasized the first three things I listed—(1)

the counsel of the Lord, (2) the condition of our souls, and (3) the condition of our communities—and then minimally gave attention to the devil.

If we will ask the first three questions of the watchman, then this next one will not be a big issue for us to deal with. Many times, though, we do not prevail against the devil because we handle his schemes in the wrong order. If we start with his schemes first, we're already on the wrong footing. As James wrote, we must first "submit to God" before we can "resist the devil" (Jas. 4:7). Before we ask a question about Satan's plan, we must ask God about His plans. Before we explore the strategies of the enemy, we need to examine our own hearts. Before we try to engage in direct spiritual warfare, we need to assess the condition of our community. Engagement with the enemy will be unsuccessful if we skip the first three important steps. If we watch in the first three areas, though, we'll automatically be fortified and equipped to deal with the fourth area.

Before moving on, let's review the first three questions and consider them within the context of spiritual warfare.

"What is God saying?" This is always the starting point. Not introspection. Not community assessment. Not Satan awareness. The word of the Lord is always first. If you skip this question, you automatically open the door to the enemy. *Self-assessment without the Lord's counsel opens the door to self-accusation.* Introspection can take a deadly turn because we're not equipped to assess ourselves properly. Though Paul charged the Church to judge herself, he also wrote something that sounds like the opposite: "I do not even judge myself. For I know of nothing against myself, yet I am not justified by this; but He who judges me is the Lord" (1 Cor. 4:3–4). Why did Paul write that he did not judge himself? Paul was explaining that *self-judgment is not accurate when it exists outside the Lord's judgment.* We will excuse ourselves too indiscriminately or condemn ourselves too quickly. Thus, the counsel of the Lord must be our beginning.

The second question we must ask ourselves is, "How am I

doing?" Without this step, we can turn the Lord's counsel into accusation toward our brother. *Without personal application first, we can use God's Word against our community, which then empowers the work of the enemy.* This happened with Peter in the garden of Gethsemane. Jesus made sure that Peter had a sword (see Luke 22:36–38). Yet He also charged Peter to watch and pray "lest [he] enter into temptation" (22:46). Because Peter didn't personally apply the commandment to watch and pray, he used his sword in a way that Jesus didn't sanction. He used it to cut off someone's ear. This is what happens when we don't first humbly apply to ourselves what God speaks to us. We take the sword He gives us and damage the people around us. Rather than causing people to hear God's Word, we do the opposite and sever their ability to hear Him. In the garden, Peter initially seemed set up for success. He was aware of the enemy, and he was equipped by Jesus. His flaw, though, was that he wasn't personally prayerful and watchful. Therefore, he was reckless in his application of what Jesus gave him. Peter skipped the step and didn't ask, "How am I doing?"

Personal surrender to the counsel of God closes doors of access to the enemy. In John 14:30, Jesus said that "the ruler of this world is coming, and he has nothing in Me." The enemy had no foothold, no access point, no crack in the door to exploit in Jesus because Jesus was perfectly submitted to the Word and will of His Father. In the same way, we close doors to the enemy when we personally embrace and apply the counsel of the Lord.

The third question is, "How are we doing?" Once we know the counsel of the Lord and apply it to ourselves, then we need to examine the condition of our community. I've found that *most spiritual warfare manifests in the space of relationships.* Personality conflicts, communication challenges, personal insecurities, and lurking envy provide lots of fodder for the enemy's plans. Concerning the last one, James wrote, "But if you have bitter envy and self-seeking in your hearts, do not boast and lie against the truth. This wisdom does not descend from above, but is earthly, sensual, demonic. For where envy and self-seeking exist, confusion and every evil thing are there" (3:14–16). *Envy creates a wide-open door to the enemy. It is "demonic." Wherever it is, "every evil thing" will show up.* As James wrote about envy, he paired it with another word: *self-seeking.* For James, the two go hand-in-hand. The reason why there is envy is because first there is self-seeking. If we only seek our own good and not the good of our community, then we eventually despise others for their successes and advancements. This rips communities apart. If, on the other hand, we embrace the communal responsibility of the watchmen, we understand that our role is to guard and improve the community, which leads to brotherly love and mutual support. We see another's advancement not as a threat, but as an answer to our prayers. So much of the enemy's activities would lose their power if we would consistently ask, "How are *we* doing?"

Aware of the Enemy

Once we ask these three questions, we are then prepared to ask the fourth, "What is the enemy attempting?" We ask this one after the other three because the first three prepare our minds to see the answer more clearly. We won't be blinded by ignorance, neglect, or ambition. *Once we know what God is saying, how we are doing personally, and how we are doing communally, we can then lift our eyes to examine external threats.*

Notice, though, how I phrased this question. I didn't write, "What is the enemy *doing*?" I wrote, "What is the enemy *attempting*?" During spiritual warfare, it's important to keep in focus our elevated position of victory and authority in Christ. God is not threatened by the enemy's plans. In fact, when He sees them, He laughs (see Ps. 2:4). Even if it *seems* the enemy's plans prosper for a season, Isaiah 54:17 describes the final reality: "No weapon formed against you shall prosper." Any weapon the enemy forms may look effective, but in the end it will backfire.

God's counsel does and will prevail. Thus, we don't ask, "What is the enemy doing?" as though he is accomplishing something. We ask, "What is the enemy attempting?" because we know that his plans are futile.

As I already described, it's important for us to be aware of the enemy's strategies. Awareness of the enemy's schemes is one of the ways in which God overthrows the enemy's schemes. God empowers His people with intel to fortify them against the enemy's assaults and harassment. When we know what the adversary is attempting, we're able to recognize it and shut the door. *Though we're not called to warfare paranoia, we are certainly called to vigilant awareness.* You find this awareness throughout Scripture. First Peter 5:8–9 says, "Be sober, be vigilant; because your adversary the devil walks about like a roaring lion, seeking whom he may devour. Resist him." Sobriety and vigilance are both watchman charges. In fact, "be vigilant" can be translated "be watchful," as in the ESV and other translations. Here the watchmen watch because the devil is lurking. As they see his plans, it equips them to "resist him." *Without awareness, though, there is no proper resistance.*

Earlier, we considered the words of Jesus, "For the ruler of this world is coming, and he has nothing in Me" (John 14:30). The enemy had nothing in Jesus. No common ground and no access point. Still, Jesus remained aware that the enemy was coming. He didn't ignore a spiritual attack just because He knew He would have victory. This perfectly models what our stance toward Satan ought to be. We should emphasize personal surrender to God primarily, but stay aware of a roaming, approaching enemy. Both warfare paranoia and warfare ignorance are destructive. *Jesus modeled warfare awareness without collapsing into warfare fixation.*

If we completely ignore the enemy, we put ourselves on vulnerable footing. To protect and guide us, God warns His people about the plans of the enemy. For example, God let Cain know that sin was crouching like a wild animal at the door. For Peter, Jesus let him know that Satan desired to sift him like wheat.

Proverbs 22:3 says, "A prudent man foresees evil and hides himself." When you foresee evil, you're able to hide yourself and take measures to shore up weakness. *When you don't foresee evil, you may be blindsided.*

Spiritual Military Intelligence

As you watch and ask, "What is the enemy attempting?" God is able to answer you specifically so you know the exact kind of battle you are facing. In other words, God doesn't just want to say, "An attack is coming." He wants to reveal the nature of the attack so you can use the right kind of weapons to see victory. For example, a few years ago, I had a dream about a rattlesnake being in my house. I knew when I woke up that the enemy wanted to create a lot of noise, confusion, and intimidation within my home. Therefore, I was not surprised when those symptoms started showing up in different situations. Thankfully, the dream didn't end with just a rattlesnake. I eventually crushed its head with my heel. Thus, I knew I had victory to withstand the attack and declare peace in the name of Jesus. I prayed and declared Romans 16:20, which says, "And the God of peace will crush Satan under your feet shortly." The dream revealed both the strategy of the enemy and the counsel of the Lord concerning how to deal with the enemy. *When God reveals the plans of the enemy, He empowers us with both awareness and counsel.* He shows us where to be vigilant and how to overcome.

The prophet Elisha watched in this way. In 2 Kings 6, Israel faced war with Syria. God continued to thwart Syria's plans, though, by using the watchmen.

Now the king of Syria was making war against Israel; and he consulted with his servants, saying, "My camp will be in such and such a place." And the man of God [Elisha] sent to the king of

Israel, saying, "Beware that you do not pass this place, for the Syrians are coming down there." . . . Therefore, the heart of the king of Syria was greatly troubled by this thing; and he called his servants and said to them, "Will you not show me which of us is for the king of Israel?" And one of his servants said, "None, my lord, O king; but Elisha, the prophet who is in Israel, tells the king of Israel the words that you speak in your bedroom." (2 Kings 6:8–12)

The Syrian king was frustrated, assuming someone in his midst was a spy, leaking secrets to Israel. But God was the One guiding Israel and frustrating the Syrians by revealing their plans. God gave the advantage to Israel through prophetic military intelligence.

It's interesting how the king of Israel responded to Elisha's counsel. When the prophet warned him, he didn't assume that victory was sure just because God revealed the enemy's plans. The king knew that he had to act according to that counsel and be watchful in that area. Notice 2 Kings 6:10: "Then the king of Israel sent someone to the place of which the man of God had told him. Thus he warned him, and he was watchful there, not just once or twice." When the king of Israel knew Syria was coming, he moved his army out of harm's way. Then, he set up a watchman to monitor the area. That watchman remained vigilant, "not just once or twice." This reveals how we ought to respond when God exposes the plans of the enemy. We first adjust anything that is directly in the line of fire. When danger is coming, we "hide" ourselves in that area, like Proverbs 22:3 charges. Then, we remain constantly aware of it, making sure we don't allow laxity or negligence to make us vulnerable.

Recently, our ministry team was hosting a conference in Manchester, United Kingdom. About one week before the conference, I had a dream. It was an uncomfortable dream but important because it revealed the tactics of the enemy against our team during the upcoming event. In the dream, we were in a conference setting. The atmosphere felt strange, as if something were off relationally among everyone. It seemed everyone was fighting his or her own private battle with insecurity and was offended with each other. The result was that everyone was distant. Off the platform, we didn't talk to each other very much. On the platform, we pulled ourselves together enough to execute the services, but there wasn't an ease of flow or unity among us.

When I have a dream like this, the first action I take is to write it down. Even if I don't initially understand everything about the dream, it's important to capture the details before they fly away. Then, I take it to prayer, listening to the Lord for interpretation and application for my life. Next, I discuss it with my wife so we can keep each other updated, and she may contribute to my understanding of the dream's interpretation. After that, I prayerfully consider sharing the dream with others, along with any interpretation or application I sense is relevant for them.

I knew this dream was a watchman dream, and the team needed to hear it. I first sent it to our lead pastors. It was important to begin there to make sure any further steps are submitted to spiritual authority. They wanted to share it with the whole team, so they sent it to everyone through a text message. Next, in staff meetings and prayer meetings, we discussed the dream and how it revealed the plans of the enemy against us during the conference. He wanted to attack our unity by turning each of us inward through insecurity and distant through offense. After discussing it, we then responded in prayer. We began with personal repentance for those individual areas that make us vulnerable to these kinds of attacks. Then, we prayed for unity, quoting scriptures such as Psalm 133 where unity causes the oil to flow and receives the commanded blessing.

After taking these initial steps, we continued to pray for unity leading up to the conference. During the conference, each of us remained aware of the enemy's strategy. That way, if we felt the rise of insecurity, we knew where it was coming from. If we felt the temptation to be offended, we knew what spirit was fueling that. Like the king of Israel in 2 Kings 6, we endeavored to remain watchful "not just once or twice." God revealed the strategies of the enemy so we could stay vigilant and fortify our hearts. The result of this dream was that our team remained unified throughout the conference, and we saw a prevailing atmosphere of the Holy Spirit where people's lives were changed.

When we're aware of the enemy's tactics, we can be more intentional both in our prayers and in taking practical steps to close inroads of the enemy. Paul explained this in 2 Corinthians 2:3–11. At the end of the passage, he famously wrote that "we are not ignorant of [the enemy's] devices." What catches my attention is the instruction he gave prior to this statement. His instruction was about forgiveness for someone who had sinned and suffered chastisement in the Church. Paul called them to "reaffirm [their] love to him" and "forgive and comfort him, lest perhaps such a one be swallowed up with too much sorrow" (v. 7). Paul's awareness of the enemy's tactics drove him to forgiveness and love within the community. He knew that unforgiveness and chastisement that is "too severe" become footholds for Satan to exploit. Thus, as a pastor-watchman, he called the Church to close those doors of vulnerability. As the Church did, Satan was not able to "take advantage" of them. Because Paul was aware of the enemy, he was able to pastor the Church, giving the people practical steps to be victorious in spiritual warfare.

1967 vs. 1973

In military warfare, there are a lot of insights we can glean about spiritual warfare, including the role of the watchmen. This is especially true if we compare two of modern Israel's wars: the Six Day War in 1967 and the Yom Kippur War in 1973. Though only six years apart, they were very different wars. In the Six Day War, Israel emerged as the undisputed victor, gaining both territory and renown for her military prowess. In the Yom Kippur War, Israel eventually performed well militarily, but at the outset things looked bleak. She faced a very real existential threat as Egypt and Syria attacked on two fronts. By the end of negotiations, Egypt—not Israel—regained territory lost six years earlier and restored its sense of military honor.

In his book *The Yom Kippur War*, Abraham Rabinovich analyzed what made the war in '73 so different from the one in '67. He revealed that Israel was unprepared because she had a breakdown in military intelligence. Though she could see Egyptian and Syrian troops amassing at her borders, Israel somehow remained blind to her enemies' actual strategy and intent. Because of this blindness, war surprised and devastated the nation. From a military standpoint, Israel recovered during the war to defend herself, but emotionally and politically, the war left an insoluble stain.

Military intelligence is akin to the role of watchmen. For the sake of communities, cities, and nations, watchmen need eyes to see and ears to hear the strategy and intent of the enemy. This is not to live warfare obsessed or demonically paranoid. It is to be prepared, ready, vigilant, and proactive regarding God's counsel. Otherwise, like Israel in '73, we'll be on our heels, fighting against an enemy who has already penetrated our ranks.

CHAPTER THIRTEEN

THE ANSWERS TO OUR PRAYERS

WE NEED NOT ONLY TO MAKE REQUESTS TO GOD, BUT ALSO EXPECT those requests to be answered. Therefore, we must watch for the answers to our prayers. We ought to be looking for their manifestation. Intercession is not just a spiritual discipline that keeps your compassion active. It is a weapon God wields to change your world. Sometimes, we need to be reminded of the simple reality that *prayer changes things*. Thus, when you pray, you need to ask, *"Where is God moving?"* That question keeps your eyes on the horizon, actively looking for the answers to your own prayers.

Several years ago, I had a dream that demonstrates our need to watch in this area. In the dream, my friend Brian Beasley was preaching. As he does, he made this statement: "Jesus told us to watch and pray. The problem is that no one is watching!" Though it was a short dream, it spoke to me deeply. To me, Brian represents a person of faith. He carries a spirit of faith and regularly steps out to see miracles. Brian also represents testimonies. For years, he has kept records of testimonies to remember what God has done, and that builds faith for what God wants to do. Thirdly, Brian represents a man of prayer. He has a history of personal prayer and of leading corporate prayer meetings. When you combine these three aspects of Brian, here's what I get from the dream: *Once we pray, we need to watch with eyes of faith to see God work in ways that create fresh testimonies.*

In the dream, when Brian said, "No one is watching," I knew he meant it in a very specific way. I knew he meant that people were absentmindedly praying prayers and then not actually expecting them to be answered. He meant that people were praying but not watching after they prayed for the answers to their prayers. Waking up from the dream, I was convicted by its message. I thought about how often I had done that. I had prayed, but I had not watched. I didn't truly expect the answers to show up. *If I was not watching for the answers to my prayers, then it's possible–it's likely!–that I was not actually praying in faith.* If I truly believed God answers me, then I would expect the answers to either show up or be on their way.

I have a picture of my oldest son, Jack, when he was six years old. He is sitting on a chair beside a window, watching our drive-way. Why was he doing that? My sister, Abigail, was on her way to visit for Christmas and would be arriving at any moment. Because he believed she was about to arrive, he watched for her. His faith in her arrival kept him at the window, even when she was a few minutes late.

That's what faith looks like. *Faith not only prays, but it also watches for the arrival of the answer to the prayers.* James 1:5–7 describes this watching-faith as a key ingredient to answered prayer: "If any of you lacks wisdom, let him ask of God who gives to all liberally and without reproach, and it will be given to him. But let him ask in faith, with no doubting, for he who doubts is like a wave of the sea driven and tossed by the wind. For let not that man suppose that he will receive anything from the Lord." That last statement is the one that stands out to me the most. When we ask without watching, without believing and expecting, we can't suppose we'll receive anything from the Lord. It's not because God only answers perfectly prayed prayers. It's because when the answer comes, we won't have our eyes lifted and our hearts ready to receive it. We miss the answer when it shows up.

The Answers Are Knocking

This failure to watch is found in Acts 12. The Church faced a real crisis. At the beginning of the chapter, Herod killed James, the brother of John. Then, Herod didn't stop with one execution. "And because he saw that it pleased the Jews, he proceeded further to seize Peter also" (12:3). Herod's intent was clear. To inflate his own popularity, he intended to kill Peter the way he had killed James. However, this time "constant prayer was offered to God for [Peter] by the church" (12:5). Their prayers were so effective they led to Peter's dramatic deliverance. God dispatched an angel to free Peter on the eve of his execution. Peter then made his way through the night to the house where everyone was praying.

At this point in the story, you might expect a celebration as the Church received Peter into the home. That's not what happened. First of all, no one was posted as a watchman at the house. Peter found the door shut and locked. He had to knock because no one was expecting his arrival. Next, a girl named Rhoda realized Peter was knocking at the door, and she forgot to let him in, running into the prayer meeting to report the good news. Rather than an eruption of praise, they accused her of being out of her mind. To them, it just wasn't possible for the answer to their prayers to actually come to pass. Because she insisted, they invented a theory to explain her exuberance: "So they said, 'It is his angel'" (12:15). Somehow, it seemed more believable to them that Peter's angel or spirit had left his body and visited the house rather than the obvious conclusion that God had answered their prayers. Meanwhile, Peter continued to knock. Finally, they opened the door, and "they were astonished." They were surprised because their prayers accomplished something.

This account is not just a historical description of what happened in Acts 12. It's also a parable for how we interact with prayer today. When we pray, many times we don't watch. We don't expect the answers to come. When they do come, we allow our human reasoning to dismiss, belittle, or overlook them. Or if we do eventually receive the answers to our prayers, it's only because God persists in knocking until He gets through all the layers of our unbelief. Finally, we're "astonished" that prayer works. In reality, we would see it work a lot more if we not only prayed, but also watched.

Asking, "What is God doing?" helps to balance the question, "What is the enemy attempting?" If we only ask the latter question, we live defensively. We allow the enemy to set the agenda of our prayers and the focus of our minds. When we ask the first question, it gives us a God awareness. It empowers us to be proactive within God's Kingdom. God sets the agenda of your prayers and the focus of your mind. When you look for the hand of God at work, you'll find it because God is always working. Jesus said, "My Father is always working, and so am I" (John 5:17 NLT). *If we don't see God working, it's likely because we've not looked for what He's doing.*

When you look for the hand of God at work, you'll find it in surprising ways. You'll realize He is present in moments you previously overlooked. As a watchman, this not only fills your own heart with gratitude, but you're also able to call others' attention to it. The more God-aware we are as communities, the more we're able to steward what God is doing. The more aware we are of the gifts He is giving in each day and moment, the more we're able to be faithful with those gifts.

While writing most of this book, I've been living in Manchester, UK, serving in ministry alongside my dear friends, Joe and Stacie Reeser. Our church community has contended in prayer often for revival in the city of Manchester. Stacie has a wonderful discipline of highlighting things that are easy to over-look regarding our prayers. She constantly brings up ways in which God is answering us. For example, there are regular monthly meetings where the pastors of Manchester meet and pray together. She reminds us of how unusual this kind of meeting is and how the unity of the pastors must be a precursor to a larger move of God. As we contend for greater revival, she thanks God for the current measure of revival we're seeing through the pastoral prayers, relationships, and unity. She is able to call our attention to God-happenings like this because she is watching for them.

How often do you watch for God-happenings in your city? How often do you to look for and thank God for even the smallest answers to your prayers?

I love Bill Johnson's perspective on living with a God-aware-ness and celebrating the seemingly small work of God. Rather than waiting on something big and noticeable to happen, Bill claims we should look for and celebrate even the smallest hint of God at work. In doing so, our gratitude prepares the way for more to come. Bill tells a story of how this played out in his church. He pastors Bethel Church in Redding, California, which has become a globally recognized church where God is moving in miraculous ways. When he first became the senior pastor, he and his wife, Beni, started contending for revival and leading the church in this pursuit. In the beginning, the going was tough. Not everyone was excited about this new direction. However, he noticed one Sunday night that one lady received from the Lord something unusual. God worked in her life in a supernatural way, bringing personal revival and refreshing. After the service, Bill looked at Beni and realized, "It's here." He meant that revival had arrived. It didn't have to be in everyone, yet. God's hand upon one person was still God's hand working in the church. From that moment, Bill and Beni cultivated the seed of revival, and now the move of God through Bethel Church is touching nations.

Here is the story in Bill's own words:

Beni and I accepted the invitation to be the new senior pastors of Bethel Church and began serving in that capacity in February of 1996. . . . On one of the first Sunday nights, I invited the whole church up to the front of the sanctuary. I wanted us to pray together. . . . We shared a genuine ache in our hearts for the MORE of God to fill our lives and that place. As I lifted up my voice, He came. The power of God fell in the room that night. It was beautiful. But He came noticeably on only one person. I'm not saying this woman was the only one touched by God, as He moves in subtle ways as well as in the overtly powerful demonstrations. But in this case His obvious manifestation of power fell on one person only, out of the hundreds present. She fell to the ground under the weighty presence of God, trembling under His power. Beni and I looked at each other and said, "We've got it. It is now unstoppable!" . . . Once the power of the Holy Spirit fell upon this one woman, it was like the leaven that gets kneaded into dough. Once it's in, it can't be removed. We knew that the impact of this move of God would become measurable in time. And it was.[1]

What would have happened if Bill had not asked, "What is God doing?" What if he had not been watching for the answers to his prayers? He would have overlooked the work of God because it didn't come in a large package. Instead, he was able to see and receive what God sent because he was actively looking for it.

Expectation

James 5:15 describes praying the "prayer of faith." What is the prayer of faith? A friend of mine, Winfred, asked the Lord a few years ago about faith. He already knew the definition of faith from Hebrews 11:1, but he also wanted to understand it better for himself. As he pondered and prayed for understanding, the Lord gave him one word: *expectation.* Winfred saw that faith is essentially expectation. When you believe, you expect. Thus, the prayer of faith contains expectation. After you pray, you expect the answers to come. You look for them. You watch for them.

It's so easy to fall into the trap of praying for duty's sake while not actually expecting the answers to come. We must remember, though, that prayer doesn't just keep our hearts connected to God. Prayer is the way God changes the world around us. *God wants to answer our prayers, and He wants us looking for their fulfilment.* In John 15:16, Jesus said, "You did not choose Me, but I chose you and appointed you that you should go and bear fruit, and that your fruit should remain, that whatever you ask the Father in My name He may give you." The reason Jesus "chose you and appointed you" is because He wants you to be fruitful. In His definition of fruitfulness, you receive answers to your prayers: "that whatever you ask the Father in [His] name He may give you." *Though you will walk through seasons where it seems as though the answers are not coming, don't stop watching. Keep expectation alive because God wants to answer you.*

I'll end this chapter with one more Joe and Stacie Reeser story. While Stacie certainly celebrates the smallest answers to prayers, she also doesn't accept the small answers as the fullness of God's response. Stacie has a wonderful way of being thankful while also dissatisfied. She has gratitude for what God is doing but honest frustration regarding the things He hasn't done yet. For a while, that perplexed Joe, and he explained to me how he would try to console her. Then, he realized that her frustration was a sign of faith. She was frustrated that the answers had not come yet because she *expected* God to answer her. It was not a lack of faith that made her agitated. Joe admitted that it was his lack of faith that made him complacent regarding delayed answers. Stacie was looking for the answers to her prayers and annoyed each day they didn't show up. Joe realized he wasn't looking as actively or expectantly as Stacie, and, therefore, it was easier to cope with not seeing those answers arrive.

Sometimes, a bit of healthy, faith-filled frustration isn't a bad thing. It's a sign of expectancy. It's a sign you are actually watching.

Do not just look for the enemy. Look for the hand of God at work and celebrate it when it shows up. Then, keep looking until it shows up in fullness. *The watchmen look for God,* which leads to our last area of watchfulness.

CHAPTER FOURTEEN

THE RETURN OF THE LORD

As I said at the end of the last section, the watchmen look for God. They don't just look for the counsel of God or the hand of God. They look for God Himself. They look for the personal, physical return of Jesus to the earth. We will never fully be watchmen if our eyes are not longing to see this event. We must, then, ask ourselves, *"How are we preparing for the return of the Lord?"*

Psalm 130:5–6 demonstrates how a desire to see God supersedes every other area of watching. It says, "I wait for the LORD, my soul waits, and in His word I do hope. My soul waits for the Lord more than those who watch for the morning—yes, more than those who watch for the morning." These verses articulate the intensity of desire to see God in a personal way. Though written before the birth of Jesus, they anticipated Jesus and the ultimate revelation of Him to the earth. God's arrival here was compared to the dawn. In one sense, that comparison communicated the restless desire to see Him. *Just as weary watchmen wait to see dawn and the end of their shift on the wall, so our hearts know that our vocation will only be fulfilled when we see Jesus returning on the clouds.* In another sense, the comparison to the dawn not only communicated desire, but also the nature of His return. In Revelation 22:16, Jesus describes Himself as "the Bright and Morning Star." When He comes, the long night of this present evil age will finally and fully be over. The longing and waiting of the watchmen to see this is greater than any other longing for any other thing.

It's important to explicitly discuss the return of the Lord because we live in an age that mocks its reality. Peter prophesied this mockery would happen, writing that scoffers would "come in the last days . . . and saying, 'Where is the promise of His coming?'" (2 Pet. 3:3–4). The enemy's strategy is to mock the return of Jesus. Satan wants you to feel silly, ignorant, and uneducated for believing that Jesus will return to the earth to rule as King and fulfill all the promises of His Father. Satan wants you to feel like believing in Jesus is like believing in a fairytale. It's for kids or the uninformed. If the physical return of Jesus seems fantastical to you, it's because you've been influenced by the spirit of the age.

Too often, we forget we are living in a story. It's a story that isn't yet complete. We are very much like the Pevensie children in C. S. Lewis's *The Chronicles of Narnia*. When they stumbled into Narnia's magical world, they were in awe of what they found. They didn't realize, though, that they had not just stepped into some other world. They had stepped into another story. Furthermore, they themselves were a part of that story. This realization didn't dawn on them until the Beavers quoted prophecy around the dinner table. Like the Pevensies, we are often in wonder at this new Kingdom God has graciously brought us into. We are also like them in that we don't yet realize this Kingdom has a story that is very much in progress. What's more, we ourselves have a part to play. We must hear the prophecies and know that our King is coming. The atheistic materialism of our culture has convinced us that there is no story. There is only stuff. There is only pleasure and pain, and life is nothing more than managing those two.

Success is minimizing the pain and maximizing the pleasure. *According to Scripture, there is something more. That something is an age to come where Jesus reigns as King and rewards His servants.*

Knowing this reality infuses our hearts with longing to see its manifestation in our day. Peter not only prophesied scoffers, but also instructed the Church about how to respond. He wrote that we ought to be "looking for and hastening the coming of the day of God" (2 Pet. 3:12). As watchmen, we look for it. We watch for it. Even more, we hasten it. We accelerate its arrival.

The cities in which we live are a part of the larger, unfolding story of the Lord's return. According to Zechariah 8:20–22, they play an active role in the age to come:

> Thus says the LORD of hosts: "Peoples shall yet come, inhabitants of *many cities*; the inhabitants of *one city shall go to another*, saying, 'Let us continue to go and pray before the LORD, and seek the LORD of hosts. I myself will go also.' Yes, many peoples and strong nations shall come to seek the LORD of hosts in Jerusalem, and to pray before the LORD."

As Jesus reigns from Jerusalem, "many peoples and strong nations" come to seek Him and pray before Him. This movement of nations begins through cities. One city provokes another with holy desire to *go, pray, and seek* the Lord. The inhabitants of cities initiate a global crescendo of nations in holy pursuit. *By being a watchman for your city now, you're not just protecting it from the schemes of the enemy or deferring the day of judgment. You're preparing it to be an integral part in God's future world as well as accelerating the arrival of that world.*

Prepare the Way

Contrary to popular belief, watching for the Lord's return doesn't create an escapism mentality within those who watch. Rather, it creates an energetic, missional mentality that co-labors with God to accelerate the Day of the Lord. That acceleration happens through adequate preparation for His return. God restrains the return of Jesus out of compassion, knowing that the earth is not fully ready to receive Him (see 2 Peter 3:9). As we prepare, the day draws closer. A healthy vision of His coming makes us active —not apathetic. We are active, knowing that if we prepare the way, He will come.

John the Baptist understood this about the first coming of Jesus. Through his preaching and baptisms, John prepared Israel to see Jesus. He explained it this way in John 1:31: "I did not know Him; but that He should be revealed to Israel, therefore I came baptizing with water." John preached with conviction and baptized with urgency, knowing Jesus was among them, ready to be revealed. To describe John's assignment, the Gospel of Luke quoted this prophecy from Isaiah:

> The voice of one crying in the wilderness: "Prepare the way of the LORD; make His paths straight. Every valley shall be filled and every mountain and hill brought low; the crooked places shall be made straight and the rough ways smooth; and all flesh shall see the salvation of God." (Luke 3:4–6)

God used John's voice to "prepare the way." What is the result of preparing the way? "All flesh shall see the salvation of God." *Preparation sets the stage for widespread revelation.*

Interestingly, when Luke wrote, "All flesh shall see the salvation of God," it is slightly different than the original prophecy in Isaiah. Here is what Isaiah wrote: "The glory of the LORD shall be revealed, and all flesh shall see it together; for the mouth of the LORD has spoken" (40:5). In this version, "all flesh" will see the "glory of the LORD . . . together." Isaiah prophesied about an event where all flesh simultaneously and collectively see God's glory. This didn't happen fully through John the Baptist's ministry. He prepared Israel for Jesus and initiated a process where salvation through the gospel would be preached to all nations, but the event has not yet happened where "all flesh" see "together" God's glory. I point this out because I believe John the Baptist's assignment is not done. His life ended with beheading, but his assignment to prepare the way continues through the Church. This time, though, we are preparing the way for Jesus's second coming. It's through Jesus's second coming that "all flesh . . . together" will see God's glory. As Revelation 1:7 describes, "Behold, He is coming with clouds, and every eye will see Him." When Jesus returns, "every eye will see Him," the One whose face is the glory of God (see 2 Cor. 4:6).

Without John, Jesus may have still come, but Israel would have been unprepared to see Him. In fact, those within Israel who did not receive John's message also did not receive Jesus. *Those who didn't embrace preparation remained blind to revelation.* Luke 7:30 says, "But the Pharisees and lawyers rejected the will of God for themselves, not having been baptized by [John]." It was the will of God for them to see and receive Jesus. They did neither because they didn't allow John's message to prepare the way in their hearts.

This brings us to a key component of preparing the way. God sends people to prepare, not because He *needs* the way prepared, but because He *wants* people ready to receive Him when He comes. *God uses watchmen to prepare the way for people's sake—not for His sake.* He doesn't need obstacles removed. When God used John the Baptist to fill valleys and level mountains, it was not because Jesus doesn't know how to deal with difficult terrain. Song of Solomon says this about Him: "The voice of my beloved! Behold, he comes leaping upon the mountains, skipping upon the hills" (2:8). The One who leaps upon mountains and skips upon hills doesn't need someone to create an easy path for Him.

Furthermore, if He wanted a mountain-less road, He is well able to do it Himself. Psalm 97:5 says, "The mountains melt like wax at the presence of the LORD." His presence melts mountains. Since all this is true, why did Isaiah and the gospel writers emphasize the role of John the Baptist in preparing the way? Again, it's not for God's sake. It's for our sake. We need every hindrance in us challenged and removed to see Him rightly when He comes.

I recently had a dream where I was preaching from Revelation 1:7: "Behold, He is coming with clouds, and every eye will see Him, even they who pierced Him. And all the tribes of the earth will mourn because of Him. Even so, Amen." After quoting the scripture, I then said this:

> When we see Him, what kind of tears will we cry? Will they come from godly sorrow because we are broken and repentant? Or will they come from worldly sorrow because we are weeping for all our stuff, all our sin, and all the secret treasures of our hearts? There is no doubt that every eye will see Him, but what kind of tears will we cry?

As I was preaching this, I felt a deep conviction and brokenness about the condition of my own heart. I knew that I needed to prepare myself to see Him, or my tears would be worldly sorrow tears. Like those in Revelation 18 crying for Babylon, I would be pining for all my worldly treasure rather than turning my heart in wonder to the beautiful Son of God.

You see, it's not a guarantee that everyone who sees Jesus will believe in Him. In the Gospels, seeing Jesus and receiving Jesus are two very different things. This is one of the reasons why Jesus Himself said, "And blessed is he who is not offended because of Me" (Matt. 11:6). *If we don't prepare our hearts to see Him, then we'll be offended when we see Him.* He may not look like what we expect, and He may not do what we want. Therefore, we need our hearts tenderized through repentance to receive our King.

Vigilant Servants

When we are truly anchored in the reality of His return, it drives us to ask, *"How are we preparing?"* This question applies to us and to our spheres of influence. How are we preparing our own hearts to see Him, and how are we preparing others to see Him? Our diligence to prepare wanes if we minimize His return. When we lose our expectation for His coming, our actions no longer align with His agenda. In Luke 12:45–46, Jesus said,

> But if that servant says in his heart, *"My master is delaying his coming,"* and begins to beat the male and female servants, and to eat and drink and be drunk, the master of that servant will come on a day when he is not looking for him, and at an hour when he is not aware, and will cut him in two and appoint him his portion with the unbelievers.

Here, Jesus described a servant who did something horrible. The servant beat his fellow male and female servants. He used the master's time and resources to eat, drink, and be drunk. What emboldened such behavior? Jesus clearly explained that the servant did this because he said "in his heart, 'My master is delaying his coming.'" When the servant minimized his master's return, he was unprepared for his return. Not only that, but he also acted in ways the master would have never sanctioned. *We live unprepared and unsanctioned lives when we are not watchful for the return of Jesus.*

Conversely, *when we watch expectantly for Him, we live ready for Him.* When we believe the Master is coming, we prepare our own hearts and those of others to receive Him. Jesus elaborated on this throughout Luke 12:35–40.

> Let your waist be girded and your lamps burning; and you your-selves be like men who wait for their master, when he will return

from the wedding, that when he comes and knocks they may open to him immediately. Blessed are those servants whom the master, when he comes, will find watching. Assuredly, I say to you that he will gird himself and have them sit down to eat, and will come and serve them. And if he come in the second watch, or come in the third watch, and find them so, blessed are those servants. But know this, that if the master of the house had known what hour the thief would come, he would have watched and not allowed his house to be broken into. Therefore, you also be ready, for the Son of Man is coming at an hour you do not expect.

Jesus emphatically charged His disciples to live ready for His return. Regardless of the hour, whether the "second watch" or "third watch," *Jesus expects us to expect Him. When He comes, He expects to find us "watching."* Our watching equips us with a girded waist and a burning lamp. We have a readiness to serve Him and a passion to love Him. When we don't watch, the lamp goes out, and we lose our readiness to serve.

My wife and I love to read nineteenth-century British literature. Some of our favorite authors are Charles Dickens, George Eliot, and Jane Austen. Once we finish a novel, we'll typically find a film adaptation to watch, though films rarely do justice to the original novel. These visual representations of Victorian England give a good reference point for what it may look like to watch for the master's return as a servant. Typically, the nobility and gentry have more than one house. When they leave one, the servants take measures to close that house for a season. In the 2005 film of Jane Austen's *Pride and Prejudice*, there is a scene where Mr. Bingley leaves his house in Netherfield. As he does, the servants cover all the furniture with cloth, protecting them from dust. It's a sign the master is away. Imagine if Mr. Bingley suddenly changed his mind and decided to return to Netherfield. What would he find? Would he find the servants watching the road, expecting to see their master? Would he find them bustling about, removing the furniture cloths, stoking fires, and preparing meals? Or would he find them lax and unprepared? Would he find them taking advantage of his absence, exploiting his resources and mismanaging their time?

This is the kind of example Jesus used when He described our responsibility to watch for Him in Luke 12. Because we know He is coming, we must ever have our eyes sharp, our hearts ready, and our hands active. *We prepare by awakening desire for Him in human hearts, dusting away the complacency of the world.* We also call to repentance those who have hostility toward the coming King. *Because He is coming at an hour we don't expect, we must labor as though He will come at any moment.*

Jesus posed this question to His disciples: "When the Son of Man comes, will He really find faith on the earth?" (Luke 18:8). In context, He was referring directly to those who expected the answers to their prayers and petitions. We can also apply His question to this larger theme of His physical return to the earth. When He comes, will He find servants who expect Him to show up? Will He find us active in our preparations for Him? Or will He find us surprised that He's real and that He has come? Will He find us unprepared to host Him as King?

When Jesus asked this question in Luke 18, it reminds me of the story in Acts 12 that we considered in the last chapter. When Peter showed up to the church's prayer meeting, he didn't find faith. They did not expect him to come, though they had been praying for him to come. This incident is a warning for us. *If we're not vigilant over our hearts, we will digress into prayers that contain no faith. We will perform religious ceremonies to a God we don't really believe in. We'll preach a historically real Jesus, but not a presently real Jesus with a future plan.* When He comes, what if Jesus experiences what Peter experienced in Acts 12? What if the door of the Church is shut to Him, and we are wholly astonished at His arrival?

Recently, a friend of mine named Emma told me about a dream she had as a teenager. It demonstrates our need as the

Church to hear afresh the message of the Lord's return. Here is her account of it:

> The dream was so unbelievably real. I will never ever forget it, and I was petrified by how real it felt in the moment. The Church was all playing games inside a church building. It was easy to join in. Something made me go outside where I saw a light getting brighter and brighter. I knew it was Jesus returning. I ran inside to tell everyone, but everyone just wanted to play the games instead and wouldn't listen. I ran back outside and fell to my knees. Then, I woke with my heart pounding. Again, it was so real. I've never remembered a dream like this one before.

So many things in this dream strike me. Instead of hearing about the Lord's return, we would rather play games. We would rather do what is easy and acceptable to the world around us than be interrupted and inconvenienced by the light that is coming. May the Lord bring to us the heart-pounding reality of this hour!

Longing as a Bride

Though it may be new territory for some of us to actively think and watch for the return of Jesus, it's only natural and right if you consider the Church's biblical identity as a bride. Brides look forward with anticipation to their wedding day. Furthermore, that anticipation drives them to prepare. Their longing for marriage does not paralyze them with complacency. Rather, it animates their actions, shaping the how and the what of their daily routine until the day comes. As the Church, we are betrothed, and our wedding day is yet to come. The coming Day should determine our daily rhythms and dictate what we put our focus upon.

Imagine how disconcerting it would be to a bridegroom if his bride never thought about their coming wedding day. Imagine if you yourself were engaged to someone, and that person never mentioned your upcoming wedding. Furthermore, when you did bring it up, what if he or she felt uneasy and didn't want to talk about it? You would probably question your betrothed's affection for you. You would wonder if he or she actually loved you. You would wonder if he or she regretted your engagement and wanted a way out.

What does it produce in the heart of Jesus when we do not watch for His return? Does it communicate to Him a lack of interest? A lack of love? What does it say about us when we feel uneasy about the coming Day of the Lord or when we don't want to hear about it or talk about it? Does it identify within us wayward affections that are tied to this world that is passing away?

Revelation 22:17 articulates the cry of a faithful bride: "And the Spirit and the bride say, 'Come!'" When our hearts are fully aligned with the Spirit of God, we do not shun the return of Jesus. We long for it. We desire it. We cry to Him, "Come!" *Even if His coming means cosmic shaking, we want Him to be here with us in covenantal promise.*

John used a fascinating two-word phrase in the book of Revelation: "even so." He used it twice, and both times it communicated the intensity of his desire to see Jesus regardless of the consequences for the world as he knew it. The first instance is Revelation 1:7, which I wrote about earlier. It says that, when every eye sees Jesus, "all the tribes of the earth will mourn because of Him." In response to this reality, John wrote, "Even so, Amen." In other words, even if His return causes tears throughout the earth, John still wanted to see Jesus. He would have rather seen Jesus amid tears than be without Jesus and protect his comfort. The second instance is Revelation 22:20. It says, "He who testifies to these things says, 'Surely I am coming quickly.' Amen. Even so, come, Lord Jesus!" When Jesus said that He is coming quickly, John immediately responded with enthusiasm and desire, asking Him to do what He said and come quickly. But why did

John add the phrase, "even so"? Remember that this verse occurs at the end of Revelation. John had just described the cosmic shaking that precedes the Lord's return, including the breaking of seals, the blowing of trumpets, and the emptying of bowls. The return of Jesus not only includes reward, but also judgment and wrath. And still, even in light of that, John wanted Jesus to return. Though his entire world will reel and persecution will intensify and birth pangs sharpen, he still wanted all of it to transpire sooner than later because he wanted to be with Jesus. After surveying it all, John said, "Even so, come, Lord Jesus!"

Do you have an "even so" in your vernacular? Do you want to see Jesus badly enough that it doesn't matter what measures God must take to prepare you and the world around you?

The apostle Paul described the reward that awaits those who have an "even so" on their lips. In 2 Timothy 4:8, he wrote, "Finally, there is laid up for me the crown of righteousness, which the Lord, the righteous Judge, will give to me on that Day, and not to me only but also to all who have loved His appearing." God gives "the crown of righteousness" to those who have loved the appearing of Jesus. This is not simply a reference to His first appearing, but it is also to His second appearing. This Greek word for *appearing* occurs five other times in the New Testament, each time through the hand of Paul.[1] Four out of the five times, it is a clear and indisputable reference to the second coming of Jesus:

> And then the lawless one will be revealed, whom the Lord will consume with the breath of His mouth and destroy with the brightness of His *coming*. (2 Thessalonians 2:8)

> That you keep this commandment without spot, blameless until our Lord Jesus Christ's *appearing*. . . . (1 Timothy 6:14)

> I charge you therefore before God and the Lord Jesus Christ, who will judge the living and the dead at His *appearing* and His kingdom. . . . (2 Timothy 4:1)

Looking for the blessed hope and glorious *appearing* of our great
God and Savior Jesus Christ. . . . (Titus 2:13)

Because Paul used this word most often to describe Jesus's second
coming, it's safe to apply that meaning here in 2 Timothy 4:8.
Thus, Scripture calls us to not only love the first appearing of
Jesus as we look back on the glorious work of salvation through
His death, burial, resurrection, and ascension. It also calls us to
love His second appearing when He descends as Bridegroom,
Judge, and King.

Furthermore, God not only rewards this love with the "crown
of righteousness," but also He uses this love to keep the actions of
the Church holy and aligned with His purposes. In Revelation
16:15, Jesus said, "Behold, I am coming as a thief. Blessed is he
who watches, and keeps his garments, lest he walk naked and
they see his shame." We find the repeated theme of Jesus coming
"as a thief," indicating that His return will catch most people by
surprise. It will be unexpected. He comes when most of the world
is asleep. Then, He charges us, "Blessed is he who watches." Jesus
calls us to watch for His return. Next, Jesus adds one of the results
of watching: "and keeps his garments." Revelation 19:8 describes
garments as the "acts of the saints." Thus, those who watch not
only look for something, but they also act in certain ways. They
"keep their garments," staying active to prepare themselves and
others for Jesus. The apostle Peter also connected watchfulness to
holiness. After describing the cosmic shaking that happens at the
Day of the Lord, he asked this question: "Therefore, since all these
things will be dissolved, what manner of persons ought you to be
in holy conduct and godliness . . . ?" (2 Pet. 3:11). *Staying aware and
watchful has a direct result upon our conduct. Holiness and godliness
accompany those who see themselves as a bride, longing for and
preparing for her wedding day.*

As I said at the beginning of this topic, we won't fully be
watchmen until our watching includes an expectation for the
return of Jesus. This expectation is not just for those within the

Church who happen to be interested in eschatology. It is for every-one. After explicitly describing the need for us to watch for His return in Mark 13:32–36, Jesus added this statement: "And what I say to you, I say to all: 'Watch!'" (v. 37). *We are disobedient disciples if our eyes are not looking for the return of Jesus.*

PART FOUR
THE REQUIREMENTS OF THE WATCHMEN

CHAPTER FIFTEEN

STAY AWAKE

So far, I've described the characteristics of the watchmen and six areas in which watchmen watch. Now, I'll describe the requirements of the watchmen. What is it that God requires of us to fulfill this vocation in the most fruitful way?

The first requirement of the watchman is to *stay awake*. If you think about watchmen in ancient cities, they are vigilant at all times—when others are awake *and* when others are asleep. Their distinguishing mark is vigilance at each hour, regardless of the inconvenience or discomfort. In the same way, *spiritual watchmen have a spiritual vigilance that keeps them awake and aware, even when others become spiritual sluggards.*

Because the Western Church lives in relative ease and comfort, it's a very real temptation for Christians to become sleepy. When that happens, we lose our spiritual hunger, desperation for God, missional urgency, and differentiating holiness. We get easily distracted, caught in the current of the cultural milieu. We forget the true purpose of the Church and turn it into something that serves our own interests.

I recently heard a story that convicted me deeply. I have a Persian friend who was formerly a Muslim. He and his wife gave their lives to Jesus and moved to America from Iran. He had

grown up in America, but the wife had not. The American Christian experience was a stark contrast to her life in Iran. She was
accustomed to the constant pressure of persecution, which created
both a natural and spiritual vigilance. In Iran, the Church must
stay watchful because their lives are at stake. The longer my
friend's wife attended his church, the more she found herself
becoming relaxed in her spiritual posture. Suddenly, she turned to
him during one of the services and said, "We have to go back to
Iran." He looked at her confused. She explained, "There is a
Satanic lullaby over the American church, and I feel myself
growing sleepy." She recognized the level of comfort the Western
Church enjoys has become a tool for the enemy to lull us asleep.
As watchmen, we must actively resist that lullaby.

If it isn't ease and comfort that lulls us to sleep, it can be
something else. In the Garden of Gethsemane, the disciples'
sleepiness kept them from watching. It says, "Then [Jesus] came
to the disciples and found them sleeping, and said to Peter,
'What! Could you not watch with Me one hour?" (Matt. 26:40).
Their drowsiness robbed from them the opportunity of watching
with Jesus. Luke's account gives insight as to why they slept,
saying, "When He rose up from prayer, and had come to His
disciples, He found them sleeping *from sorrow*." They must have
felt the spiritual intensity of that moment, the demonic oppres-
sion swirling around the garden. Though they didn't exactly
know all that was about to happen, their hearts sensed something
awry, and it created "sorrow" within them. Have you ever experienced this? A nameless sorrow and an oppressive atmosphere
weighing upon you? How do you respond? If you're like me, it
can produce a paralyzing lethargy. It is difficult to get out of bed
or find motivation to pray. Unfortunately, we often allow despon-
dency to shut our eyes to spiritual realities. As watchmen,
though, it is our responsibility to turn individual sorrow into an
opportunity for greater intimacy with God. Though Paul experienced immense personal pain, he still wanted to know Christ in
"the fellowship of *His* sufferings" (Phil. 3:10). *Rather than allowing*

affliction to push Paul inward, it motivated him into greater relationship with God.

After finding them asleep the first time, Jesus comes a second time. Matthew 26:43 says, "He came and found them asleep again, for their eyes were heavy." He again roused them, but then found them a third time in the same condition. Jesus responded, "Are you still sleeping and resting? Behold, the hour is at hand" (26:45). The repetition of Jesus waking them reveals just how much He wanted them with Him and prepared for what lie ahead. Because they didn't know the hour that was "at hand" they assumed they could sleep and not miss too much. They assumed Jesus would still be there when they finally woke up. That wasn't the case, though. They missed the opportunity to know His sorrow at a unique moment in human history.

When we allow ourselves to drift from vigilance, it's because we don't really know the hour in which we live. We don't know what is "at hand." Also, we assume God will always be available in the same way and we're not missing too much by disengaging. We don't realize that we're missing the opportunity to co-labor with His suffering in unique ways today. The disciples never again had the opportunity to watch with Him in that hour. There would be other opportunities and other situations, but not that one. They missed the Garden of Gethsemane moment, and Jesus had to sweat great drops of blood alone.

This was not the first time drowsiness impaired their ability to see what was happening right in front of them. On the Mount of Transfiguration, sleepiness almost stole that moment, too. Jesus was on the mountain with Peter, James, and John. As He prayed, Moses and Elijah appeared in glory and spoke with Jesus. As all this unfolded, the disciples almost missed it, and Luke explained why: "But Peter and those with him were heavy with sleep; and when they were fully awake, they saw His glory and the two men who stood with Him" (Luke 9:32). As long as they were "heavy with sleep," they couldn't see what was happening in glory. It wasn't until they were "fully awake" that they could see. It's the same lesson from the Garden of Gethsemane: For us to watch, we must *stay awake*.

When I urge you to "stay awake," I'm referring primarily to spiritual vigilance. *When you are spiritually awake and aware, then your heart can perceive God, even when your body is resting.* I love this verse from Song of Solomon 5:2: "I sleep, but my heart is awake; it is the voice of my beloved!" It's possible for your body to be relaxed, but your heart to be vigilant. In Song of Solomon, it's the Shulamite's love that kept her heart attentive to the Beloved's voice. Because she loved him, she wanted to hear him. In the same way, *it's our love for Jesus that keeps our hearts attentive to Him. When we are consumed with love for Him, we can't imagine abandoning friendship with Him and not watching with Him.* David wrote something similar in Psalm 63:6: "When I remember You on my bed, I meditate on You in the night watches." When he rested at night, his thoughts went toward God. Because of this, his meditation remained on God, even through the night. His body was asleep, but his heart was awake. Perhaps, this is why he could write in Psalm 16:7, "My heart also instructs me in the night seasons." Because his heart was awake to God even in the night, it was able to receive instruction from God during the night. *David was able to maintain prophetic sensitivity because he didn't disengage from spiritual vigilance just because his body was resting.*

When we spiritually sleep, we miss opportunities for fellowship with God and access to His counsel. Furthermore, we make ourselves and others vulnerable to the enemy. In Matthew 13, Jesus taught the parable of the wheat and the tares. The wheat are the "sons of the kingdom," who carry out God's righteous agenda in the earth. The tares are the "sons of the wicked one," who attempt to disrupt God's plan and diminish the light of righteousness. The surprising thing about the parable is that the tares are mingled among the wheat. There is not a "wheat" field and then a "tares" field. They co-exist in the same location, growing together, side by side. The beginning of the parable explains how this happens: "The kingdom of heaven is like a man who sowed good seed in his field; *but while men slept,* his enemy came and sowed tares among the wheat" (Matt. 13:24–25). The enemy came at a precise time: "while men slept." *When we sleep, we give the enemy opportunity to sow tares into our lives and communities. When we're awake, we can see what the enemy is attempting and protect ourselves and others.*

Proverbs 24:30–34 also describes the negative impact of spiritual sloth. It describes how a vineyard becomes overgrown internally and vulnerable externally through the neglect of its owner. That neglect is directly linked to sleepiness:

> I went by the field of the lazy man, and by the vineyard of the man devoid of understanding; and there it was, all overgrown with thorns; its surface was covered with nettles; its stone wall was broken down. When I saw it, I considered it well; I looked on it and received instruction; a little sleep, a little slumber, a little folding of the hands to rest; so shall your poverty come like a prowler, and your need like an armed man.

The vineyard was "overgrown with thorns." That's internal neglect. Also, its "stone wall was broken down." That's external neglect. What is the cause? "A little sleep, a little slumber." Internally, there were thorns, weeds, and tares. Externally, the "stone wall" no longer formed a sufficient barrier of protection. This condition comes about when sleep and slumber weaken our diligence. *As watchmen, we can't afford to disengage and leave our post. If we do, thorns grow in the Lord's vineyard, and there is no stone wall of intercession to withstand the enemy.*

Practical Steps to Stay Awake

What is one of the causes of spiritual drowsiness, and is there anything we can do to avoid it? Jesus gave us an insight in Luke

21: "But take heed to yourselves, lest your hearts be weighed down with carousing, drunkenness, and cares of this life, and that Day come on you unexpectedly . . . . Watch therefore . . ." (vv. 34–36). Jesus warned about different activities that distract us from watching: "carousing, drunkenness, and cares of this life." When we don't "take heed" to ourselves regarding each of these, our hearts are "weighed down." Like Peter in the Garden of Gethsemane and on the Mount of Transfiguration, we are heavy with sleep.

I particularly like the way the King James Version translates Luke 21:34: "And take heed to yourselves, lest at any time your hearts be overcharged with surfeiting." The first time I read this, I had to look up the word *surfeiting* because it was unfamiliar to me. It means to suffer from the effects of overindulgence.[1] Those effects certainly include discomfort or sleepiness. For Americans, it's what we know as the Thanksgiving effect. After indulging in rich foods, including turkey and dressing, most people need an afternoon nap. We are *surfeited* with Thanksgiving dinner. Now, consider how the Thanksgiving effect applies to other areas of our lives. How often are our spiritual senses blunted because we overindulge in activities that are not God-oriented? I'm not claiming that all those activities are intrinsically evil. However, anything pushed to an intemperate amount can induce lethargy. Overindulgence leads to being "overcharged." Our hearts are so full with so many other thoughts and activities that there is no more space or capacity for God's work and desires. According to Jesus, if we don't "take heed" to ourselves, this can happen "at any time." We are vulnerable in this area, especially in a Western society where there is so much abundance.

What can we do to guard ourselves against surfeiting? First of all, Paul listed "temperance" as a fruit of the Spirit in Galatians 5:23 (KJV). Other translations use "self-control." *When we are filled, led by, and sensitive to the Spirit, He keeps our appetite in check.* This is not an area where God leaves us on our own, hoping that we get it right someday. He Himself is with us by His Spirit, guiding our hearts away from being "overcharged."

Secondly, I recommend fasting. *When you fast, it breaks your addiction to overindulgence. It dethrones the "god of your belly" and communicates to your soul where your true hunger lies.* Fasting sharpens your spiritual senses and keeps your mind awake. There are a variety of ways to fast, and I recommend finding a rhythm to incorporate it into your life on a regular basis. When you fast, you counteract the lethargy that results from satiety.

My wife has a lot of stories about me getting very sleepy while driving. During our dating years and early marriage, we traveled with a ministry team. We would often be on the road during the weekends, driving late at night. She typically would be more alert than me, able to keep her eyes vigilantly on the road. It was both embarrassing and dangerous how quickly and easily I would succumb to sleepiness. It wasn't until years later that I discovered a major factor contributing to my getting tired: food. Usually, just before we would hit the road, we would eat a big meal at the church where we had ministered. Then, we would stop at a gas station to buy snacks for the drive. In my mind, all these snacks were ways to stay awake. I realized later they were having the opposite effect. Rather than keeping me awake, they were taking me under. When my belly is full, my eyes get heavy. Since then, I've made changes, and I'm amazed at how easily I'm able to drive late at night now. A simple adjustment with food has had a direct impact on my ability to stay awake.

Just after moving to Manchester, I received a prophetic word from a friend. He texted me, "The Lord said you will have to be disciplined in fasting in this new season you are in. It will be your key to not getting sucked into the spiritual climate. . . . The dullness of the spiritual climate will try to lull you asleep and will be subtle. Guard your awakened heart." As in America, the UK also has spiritual forces that try to blunt the vigilance of the Church. (And that's probably true in each nation, expressed in different cultural variations.) Through this word, God was giving me counsel on how to resist negative acclimation. Rather than become accustomed to Manchester's spiritual climate, I must fast to guard my heart. For you, the same counsel applies. *Watchmen are constantly in danger of allowing the spiritual climate around them to dictate their level of spiritual awareness.* Instead of succumbing to what feels natural, fasting is an adverse action that keeps you alert and awake. *God doesn't send you to a city to become a normal resident of the city. He sends you to a city with a mission in mind, and you must fight to remind yourself of that.*

This endeavor to stay awake is part of our calling as watchmen. If we're not awake and aware, then we won't be able to see what is on the horizon, and we won't be able to use our voices to notify and awaken others. Matthew 25 emphasizes how important it is for the watchmen to stay awake. Jesus told the story of the ten virgins who were expecting the bridegroom. Five were foolish, and five were wise regarding the oil they prepared in their lamps. There is a trait, though, that unites all ten of them: They all slept. "But while the bridegroom was delayed, they all slumbered and slept" (25:5). What changed their condition as the bridegroom approached? "And at midnight a cry was heard: 'Behold, the bridegroom is coming; go out to meet him!'" (25:6). There was a cry at midnight that awakened the slumbering wedding party. That cry came from the lone watchman who stayed awake while everyone else slept. Because he kept his eyes on the horizon, expecting the bridegroom's coming, he was able to use his voice to awaken others.

We must be awake and stay awake to be the watchmen God calls us to be. This includes taking practical steps to guard our hearts from surfeiting. It also includes asking God to keep our spiritual senses awake so we don't become dull. In Zechariah 4, the prophet recorded an interesting encounter. He wrote, "Now the angel who talked with me came back and wakened me, as a man who is wakened out of his sleep" (4:1). An angel wakened Zechariah, but it wasn't a mere physical or natural awakening. It's clearly a spiritual awakening because he used the simile "as a man who is wakened out of his sleep." The spiritual awakening was so significant, it made his prior spiritual condition look like sleep. Next, the angel asked him, "What do you see?" (4:2). Zechariah was awakened to watch. The purpose behind his wakening was to see something and release it to others. This is the kind of work God wants to do in us. He wants to awaken us and equip us to watch. Even when we are already active in prophetic sensitivity, He wants to bring us into a new degree of wakefulness. This encounter with the angel was not Zechariah's first introduction to him. Notice that Zechariah 4:1 begins, "Now the angel who talked with me came back." The prophet already had experience with him, but the angel "came back" to do a fresh work. God had more to say to Zechariah, and He needed him keenly awake to receive it.

This Zechariah experience gives a good framework for the way of the watchmen. Though we may have history with God, we embrace a fresh awakening to sharpen our eyes and sound our voices. We endeavor to be and stay fully awake, heeding Paul's charge in 1 Thessalonians 5:6, "Therefore let us not sleep, as others do, but let us watch and be sober."

CHAPTER SIXTEEN

STAY FOCUSED

THE NEXT REQUIREMENT OF THE WATCHMEN IS TO *STAY FOCUSED*. When God reveals something to us by His Spirit, we must capture our attention in a way that sustains focus upon it. If we merely glance at it, then we won't experience the full reason for which God revealed it. We may have a glimmer of insight into the Spirit, but we won't mature through the development of prophetic sensitivity, intercessory love, and missional obedience. Thus, we won't see the full measure of change God intended through us.

Ezekiel 40:4 is one of my favorite scriptures that calls the watchmen to sustained focus. It says, "And the man said to me, 'Son of man, look with your eyes and hear with your ears, and fix your mind on everything I show you; for you were brought here so that I might show them to you. Declare to the house of Israel everything you see.'" In this encounter, God called Ezekiel to do something more than just see and hear. He called Ezekiel to "fix [his] mind" upon what he saw and heard. Once Ezekiel saw something, he needed to continue gazing upon it. Once he heard something, he had to meditate upon what he heard, replaying it in his mind. He had to have a holy fixation upon the things of God. From that place of sustained focus, Ezekiel could properly "declare" what he had seen. *Without sustained attention upon it, what he declared would most likely have been partial, incomplete, and immature.*

In the book of Revelation, John frequently used a word combination that captures this idea of sustained focus. He wrote, "I looked, and behold. . ." (Rev. 4:1 and others). In the NKJV, this combination is used ten times in Revelation. In each instance, John called the reader beyond a casual consideration of what he was describing. He didn't want us to merely read what he wrote. He wanted us to "behold" it. He wanted us to gaze upon it and see it for ourselves. He wanted us to fix our minds upon it. John wanted us to do this because he himself had done this. The book of Revelation isn't a glance into heavenly realities. It's a complex picture that wasn't fully painted until John sustained his gaze upon what the Spirit was showing him. John lived what Paul the apostle charged in Colossians 3:2 when he wrote, "Set your mind on things above." When you "set your mind," it's not an occasional drift into the things of the Spirit. You intentionally take the reins of your imagination and direct it toward the things of heaven. You "behold" the open door through which God is calling you.

There is a battle for our focus. We live in a world filled with screens, clamoring for our attention. In one sense, we have trained our minds to never have sustained focus upon anything. We quickly move between apps, shifting our attention from category to category. We've become proficient at maneuvering the mind's eye through an array of content. We take full advantage of having instant access to entertainment and communication. In doing so, we've trained ourselves to just keep moving the moment we feel the slightest twinge of boredom. In another sense, though we don't sustain focus upon anything particularly, we do have sustained focus upon something generally. That general focus is upon the trite distraction readily available to us. It has become a way of life to set our minds on nothing and everything—that is, everything except the things of the Spirit. *If our bodies are surfeited with food, our minds are surfeited with screens.* Our mental appetite is "overcharged," and we lack the bandwidth to think upon, meditate upon, and gaze upon God.

Though it will convict us, we need to hear Paul's words in Philippians 3:19. He listed the characteristics of those who are enemies of the cross of Christ. Within that list, he described those "who set their mind on earthly things." This is a shocking characteristic because you would imagine the enemies of the cross to have outrageous behavior, displaying outright hostility toward God. Instead, Paul described them as simply having a wayward gaze. They set their mind on earthly things. This convicts me when I consider how much I do this very thing. Rather than living Colossians 3:2 ("set your mind on things above"), I often live Philippians 3:19, setting my mind on earthly things. When I do that, I'm in danger of living averse to God's plan and opposed to the sacrifice He calls me to make. Therefore, I often pray Psalm 119:37, which says, "Turn away my eyes from looking at worthless things, and revive me in Your way." The relevancy of this prayer for our world today is stunning. Our eyes ever rove, surveying the "worthless things" this world offers us. Through His grace, God can "turn" our eyes and capture our gaze. The psalmist prayed for this, and we can, too. Furthermore, the more frequently you pray this prayer, the more likely you are to embrace and implement its answer. It would feel quite hypocritical to ask God to turn your eyes from worthless things and then intentionally waste hours looking at worthless things. When you pray Psalm 119:37, the prayer becomes a point of awareness that is itself part of the answer to the prayer.

A. W. Tozer described the need for sustained focus for our growth in God. He wrote, "We must practice the art of long and loving meditation upon the majesty of God."[1] His word choice in this sentence helps us grapple with the task in front of us. He used "practice" because it will require effort. Fixing our attention upon God may not come naturally at first because we've trained our minds to do otherwise. Tozer admitted this, writing, "This will take some effort. . . . The focal point of man's interest is now himself. . . . All this must be reversed by a deliberate act of the will and kept so by a patient effort of the mind."[2] Through "patient effort" and "practice," we can find a new habit of mind which meditates upon God.

Not Always Labor

Once we truly catch glimpses of God, sustaining our gaze toward Him becomes easier and easier. Focus is not ever doomed to be a laborious task. Consider the heavenly beings Ezekiel described in his encounters. One of the features that intrigues me the most is their number of eyes. They do not merely have eyes in their faces. Their eyes cover their entire bodies. Ezekiel said, "And their whole body, with their back, their hands, their wings, and the wheels that the four had, were full of eyes all around" (10:12). When John saw the four living creatures in Revelation, he described the same feature: "And in the midst of the throne, and around the throne, were four living creatures full of eyes in front and in back" (4:6). With that many eyes, imagine how easy it would be to succumb to distraction. With only two eyes, humans have a difficult time keeping themselves focused. Imagine how distracted we would be with eyes pointing in every direction. These living creatures, though, have a sustained gaze. John said, "The four living creatures . . . were full of eyes around and within. And they do not rest rest day or night, saying: 'Holy, holy, holy, Lord God Almighty, who was and is and is to come!'" (Rev. 4:8). They stay awake, and they stay focused. They "do not rest day or night," and with their vigilance they keep their eyes fixed on God, ever worshipping Him. They have a simple and fiery obsession with God.

Tozer contrasted their God obsession with our chronic distraction here on earth. He explained, "If some watcher or holy one who has spent his glad centuries by the sea of fire were to come to earth, how meaningless to him would be the ceaseless chatter of the busy tribes of men."[3] The first time I read that sentence from Tozer I was immediately convicted. I know of no better phrase to describe our condition than "the ceaseless chatter of the busy tribes of men." It's important to note that Tozer wrote that in 1961, a few decades before the development of smart phones and social media. He was writing not to a technological situation, but a basic human tendency to busy ourselves with everything except God. Describing that tendency, he said, "We have lost our spirit of worship and our ability to withdraw inwardly to meet God in adoring silence. . . . The words, 'Be still, and know that I am God,' mean next to nothing to the self-confident, bustling worshiper in this middle period of the twentieth century."[4] *We are "bustling" and busy, looking everywhere except heavenward.* Thus, Tozer quoted these words from Anselm to confront us and invite us into different habit of mind:

> Up now, slight man! Flee for a little while thy occupations; hide thyself for a time from thy disturbing thoughts. Cast aside now thy burdensome cares, and put away thy toilsome business. Yield room from some little time to God, and rest for a little time in Him. Enter the inner chamber of thy mind; shut out all thoughts save that of God and such as can aid thee in seeking Him.[5]

As watchmen, it is not irresponsible to "flee" and "hide" from "occupations" and "disturbing thoughts" that pull our eyes away from God. *Keeping our eyes on Him is the most responsible thing we can do.* As we carve out time to spend with God in "long and loving meditation" upon Him, then we'll develop a new habit of mind that stays with us beyond the cloistered environment of a prayer closet.

Remember how my watchmen dream ended? I was grieved because the Church experienced the whirlwind but didn't embrace the interruption and fix their minds upon it. They didn't sustain their focus upon what God had showed them. They heard

God. They experienced God. But they did not gaze upon God to fully digest, understand, and implement the encounter.

Conversely, remember how Ezekiel responded when he first experienced the whirlwind? He sat by the River Chebar "astonished" for seven days. His encounter became an interruption that redirected his focus. Because of that, Ezekiel did not simply tell stories about the whirlwind. He understood the whirlwind as a call from God that catapulted him into a new lifestyle. *The whirlwind had full fruitfulness through Ezekiel because he fixed his mind upon it.* May we follow Ezekiel's example and set our minds upon the things of God.

CHAPTER SEVENTEEN

STAY PURE

THE THIRD REQUIREMENT OF THE WATCHMEN IS TO *STAY PURE*. OUR hearts must stay awake. Our minds must stay focused. And our eyes must stay pure.

In Ezekiel 44, Ezekiel's vision of a new Temple continued. As it did, he saw a curious detail about the eastern gate: "Then He brought me back to the outer gate of the sanctuary which faces toward the east, but it was shut" (44:1). God then explained to him why the gate was shut: "And the LORD said to me, 'This gate shall be shut; it shall not be opened, and no man shall enter by it, because the LORD God of Israel has entered by it; therefore it shall be shut'" (44:2). The gate was shut and inaccessible because God Himself had used the eastern gate.

When I first read this scripture years ago, it became a rallying point for me in regard to purity. When I read about the eastern gate, God emphasized to me the "gates" of my own life: my eyes, my ears, and my mind. Through these three gateways, content enters my life that either accelerates me toward God or pulls me away from Him. *What I look upon, what I listen to, and what I think about have a direct impact upon what fills my life. With these gates, I can either give Satan access, or I can give God access.* My friend

Samuel had a similar revelation from Isaiah 28:6. It describes how God will strengthen "those who turn back the battle at the gate." From this scripture, Samuel began to battle for his gates, being zealous for his eyes and ears to be set upon the things of God.

In Ezekiel 44, the gate is shut not just in anticipation of God using it, but in response to God having used it. It doesn't say, "This gate shall be shut because God *will* enter by it." It says, "This gate shall be shut . . . because the LORD God of Israel *has* entered by it." *The gate's consecration was a response to God's activity.*

Preliminary and Responsive Consecration

There is precedent in Scripture for both preliminary consecration and responsive consecration. In Joshua 3:5, you see preliminary consecration. It says, "And Joshua said to the people, 'Sanctify yourselves, for tomorrow the LORD will do wonders among you.'" For God to do wonders among them, they had to sanctify themselves, taking specific steps to be prepared for the work of God. In other scriptures, such as Ezekiel 44:2, you see responsive consecration. The eastern gate was consecrated *because* God had used it. God's activity had set the gate apart, making it holy and unusual. The eyes of the watchmen fall into both categories: preliminary and responsive consecration.

In one sense, Ezekiel's consecration prepared the way for God to visit him in the whirlwind. Ezekiel 1:3 says that "the word of the LORD came expressly to Ezekiel *the priest*." Ezekiel was a priest, a part of the consecrated tribe of Levi. They belonged to the Lord in a special way, living by a different standard than the other tribes in Israel. In another sense, though, Ezekiel's consecration was a response to the whirlwind. In Ezekiel 3:17, God says to him, "I have made you a watchman." Becoming a watchman was not something Ezekiel achieved or accomplished. God did the work.

He made Ezekiel a watchman, and the rest of his life was spent in response to that work.

Keeping our eyes pure and consecrated is easiest when we embrace these two aspects. *We guard our gates because we anticipate God using them. We anticipate God speaking to us and revealing to us His heart. We don't want anything to detract or distract us from hearing and seeing Him. And when God does reveal Himself to us, we respond by guarding that work. We honor His revelation to us by protecting the avenues He has used as gateways.*

You see, *once God touches something, it is no longer fit to be used for other things.* It belongs to Him. In Genesis 32, Jacob wrestled with God. During the wrestling match, God dislocated Jacob's hip: "Now when He saw that He did not prevail against him, He touched the socket of his hip; and the socket of Jacob's hip was out of joint as He wrestled with him" (32:25). As a result, Jacob walked with a limp. Additionally, the children of Israel treat differently that muscle on animals they eat. Genesis 32:32 says, "Therefore to this day the children of Israel do not eat the muscle that shrank, which is on the hip socket, because He touched the socket of Jacob's hip in the muscle that shrank." Because God touched it, they don't eat it. They consider it the Lord's portion. This is responsive consecration. God touched it, so it's now His. They must handle it differently.

Once God uses your eyes as watchmen eyes, they're different. You can't use them in the same way. Before that, you may have been able to gaze upon worldly things. Now, they are the Lord's, and you must treat them accordingly. Like the eastern gate, when temptation knocks, the door must remain shut because it is the Lord's. When I first read Ezekiel 44:2, God impressed upon my heart, "I use your eyes, ears, and mind to speak you. They must remain shut to everything else." This is a much more inspiring motivation than just responding to temptation, "I really shouldn't." When you have a vision for how God wants to use the gates of your life, you are much more likely to guard them. When the enemy tries to lure your eyes, it's much easier to respond, "These are watchmen's eyes," than just saying, "No."

The moral vision of the world endeavors to be good for goodness' sake alone. In 2008, the American Humanist Association launched a bus campaign with the slogan, "Why believe in God? Just be good for goodness' sake."[1] While Christians disagree with that statement philosophically, the attitude in which we pursue holiness has a practical similarity. *Too often, Christians endeavor to be good, pure, and holy without a vision driving that pursuit.* Like the anti-drug use campaign of the '80s and '90s, we try to fortify against temptation with the slogan, "Just Say No." Ezekiel 44 offers a better way.

First, Ezekiel 44 identified the eastern gate as the Lord's. Next, it described what the eastern gate should be used for: "As for the prince, because he is the prince, he may sit in it to eat bread before the LORD" (44:3). The exact identity of "the prince" is a matter of debate. Though we may speculate who that is, we don't have to speculate what he did in the eastern gate. He used it to "eat bread before the LORD." This consecrated gate could only be used for communion with the Lord. Any other use was inappropriate. This is the vision that should drive our battle at the gates. We fight for our gates in anticipation of God using them, because God uses them, and because we are protecting our communion with Him. *We refuse to tolerate anything that could interrupt the flow of friendship and conversation with God.*

The Cycle of Purity

Other verses testify to this motivation as well. Hebrews 12:14 charges us, "Pursue peace with all people, and holiness, without which no one will see the Lord." *Holiness and peace precede seeing Jesus.* As Jesus said in Matthew 5:8, "Blessed are the pure in heart, for they shall see God." *Purity precedes seeing Him.* First John 3:2–3 says, "We know that when He is revealed, we shall be like Him, for we shall see Him as He is. And everyone who has this hope in Him purifies himself, just as He is pure." These verses first explain that seeing Jesus transforms us. When we see Him, we become like Him. Next, the verses describe what people do who actually believe that. They purify themselves. Why? Because purity precedes a full revelation of Jesus. Then, the full revelation of Jesus leads to purity. It is the process of pursuit that fuels the cycle of purity.

1. We purify ourselves in anticipation of seeing Him.
2. We see Him, and it changes us.
3. Then, we guard our gates because He used them to reveal Himself.
4. Because we guard our gates, He uses them to reveal Himself again.
5. When we see Him, it changes us . . .

And on and on the cycle goes.

David modeled this rhythm. In Psalm 27:4, he described his desire to "behold the beauty of the LORD." In Psalm 101:3, he wrote, "I will set nothing wicked before my eyes." Though these verses are in different psalms, they are not separate activities. *Those who want to behold the Lord also turn their eyes from wicked things. It's not appropriate to use them for both gazing at God and gazing at wickedness.*

Describing a different member of the body, the tongue, James explained how odd it is to use the same organ in polar opposite ways: "But no man can tame the tongue. It is an unruly evil, full of deadly poison. With it we bless our God and Father, and with it we curse men, who have been made in the similitude of God. Out of the same mouth proceed blessing and cursing. My brethren, these things ought not to be so" (James 3:8–10). Imagine if James also wrote a passage about the way we use our eyes. It may read, "With them we behold God, and with them we behold the very things that grieve God. Into the same eyes we invite revelation and invite temptation. These things ought not to be so!"

There is a battle for your eyes. When you identify them as a watchman's eyes, as the Lord's gates, as corridors of communion and revelation, you are much more likely to win the battle. You fight to stay pure when you truly believe that you will see the Lord. As watchmen, that is our greatest desire.

PART FIVE
THE RHYTHMS OF THE WATCHMEN

CHAPTER EIGHTEEN
BUZI

In my watchman dream, after I prophesied a direct, authoritative message about God looking for watchmen and how that impacts cities, I said something quite unusual. I told the men to pay attention to someone's name who starts with a "B" because it would teach them about being a watchman. To be honest, that part of the dream was the most mysterious to me, and after having the dream, I was tempted to dismiss it because I didn't see its immediate relevance. The more I have considered it and studied Scripture, though, the more convinced I am that it's part of the message God wants us to hear and apply. It's important to embrace what God speaks to you even when you don't understand it, rather than only embracing what you immediately have a paradigm for receiving. The next four chapters are my attempt at understanding and applying this mysterious element of the dream. As you read, it will provide further reference points for the nuances and rhythms within the life of a watchman.

I knew the "B" man was either in the book of Ezekiel or somehow connected to the book of Ezekiel. As I've prayerfully pondered this, I discovered several possibilities to consider. Within the book of Ezekiel, there is a clear candidate for who that person is, but several other people outside Ezekiel have caught my eye as well. I've wonder if this multiple choice "B" man is God's way of emphasizing different rhythms of the watchmen lifestyle. God is more than capable of revealing a specific, singular person if He desires. Think about how specific and clear it was that nine cities in the west of Israel faced destruction. Perhaps, He kept this part vague so I would consider more than one person as a possibility, enlarging my understanding of the watchman call. Therefore, I want to look at each of these men because they each have something to teach us about the rhythm and the results of a watchman lifestyle.

The first person to consider is Buzi. He appears at the outset of Ezekiel: "The word of the LORD came expressly to Ezekiel the priest, *the son of Buzi*, in the land of the Chaldeans by the River Chebar; and the hand of the LORD was upon him there" (1:3). Ezekiel was "the son of Buzi." Thus, it would be quite irresponsible to overlook Buzi as the possible "B" man. Buzi means "my contempt."[1] We could say, as names are always important in Scripture and often offer insight, Ezekiel was "the son of contempt." That doesn't sound very encouraging, but what can it teach us about the watchman lifestyle?

Watchmen are needed in hours of great desperation. They are needed when people have shown contempt for God and are in danger of being shown contempt by God. In 1 Samuel 2:30, God said, "Those who honor Me I will honor, and those who despise Me shall be lightly esteemed." One of the ways to translate "lightly esteemed" is to "bring into contempt."[2] Though God is long-suffering toward man, if we perpetually show contempt for God, the day will come when He will show contempt for us. If we continually reject God, then He will reject us. If we despise God, then He will despise us. Ezekiel was called by God to be a watchman in a moment such as this.

The hand of the Lord came upon Ezekiel in the "land of the Chaldeans." Though Ezekiel was a priest, he was not in Jerusalem. He was not in the Temple. He was in exile. Why? Because Israel and Judah continually despised God through their idolatry and adultery, they were "lightly esteemed." Nebuchad-nezzar laid siege to Jerusalem, took her inhabitants captive, and eventually razed the city to the ground. Remember, this didn't happen rashly at Israel's first offense. Neither did it happen without warning. As 2 Chronicles 36:15–16 explains, God "sent warnings" that they "mocked . . . despised . . . and scoffed at." Because they "despised His words," they experienced the reality of 1 Samuel 2:30. They despised God and found themselves despised by God.

It would have had particular resonance with the Jewish people to know that Nebuchadnezzar took them to the "land of the Chaldeans." According to Genesis 15:7 and Nehemiah 9:7, that was the land *from which* God took Abraham. It was from there that God separated Abraham (and thus, Israel), calling him His own. Returning to the land of the Chaldeans must have felt as though Israel's unique election was in jeopardy.

What's more, the land of the Chaldeans can also be referred to as "the land of Shinar," as in Daniel 1:2. Again, that would have had particular resonance with Judah and Israel. According to Genesis 11:2, the Tower of Babel was built in the land of Shinar. Thus, the inhabitants of Jerusalem, such as Daniel and Ezekiel, were forced from the God chosen city and then living in the confusion and chaos of the nations. Like the nations at the Tower of Babel, they were living scattered by God.

It's within this bleak environment God called Ezekiel. He took a son of contempt and made him a watchman for his people, his city, and his nation. Why did God do this? Though His judgment made it seem as if He despised Israel, in reality His steadfast love endured. Though it seemed He had utterly forsaken the nation, He wouldn't leave them alone. Ezekiel means "God strengthens." Through the watchmen, God strengthens those who are sons of contempt. *To those living in a desperate hour, God has something to say through His watchmen. They will be honest in their assessment of sin, but they will also inject hope into those who are willing to repent.*

As a "son of contempt," Ezekiel described a devastating

vision. In Ezekiel 10, he watched the glory depart from the Temple. The people of God had lost their distinguishing mark, which was the presence of God. As the glory departed, all the judgments God warned them about ensued. After all, according to Deuteronomy 31:17, it's the absence of God's presence that brings calamity: "And many evils and troubles shall befall them, so that they will say in that day, 'Have not these evils come upon us because our God is not among us?'" When God is not among them, "evils and troubles" plague their land. Though this vision was quite troubling, Ezekiel's prophecy didn't stop there. He wasn't just a "son of contempt." He was also Ezekiel, "God strengthens." Through him, God strengthened with hope those He had just chastened. In the next chapter, God spoke to Ezekiel, saying, "Therefore, say, 'Thus says the Lord GOD: "Although I have cast them far off among the Gentiles, and although I have scattered them among the countries, yet I shall be a little sanctuary for them in the countries where they have gone"'" (11:16). The glory departed from the Temple, but it traveled with them into exile.[3] Though they may not have felt it or recognized it, God's presence continued to cover them as "a little sanctuary" in the chaos and confusion of Shinar.

What does Buzi teach us about being a watchman? Don't be surprised if God calls you at times and in places where intercession is desperately needed. Don't be surprised if you live in the colliding realities of despair and hope. Don't be surprised if you sound schizophrenic, at one moment describing God's wrath and at another moment describing His unfailing love. Through watchmen, God wants to confront and yet strengthen the sons of contempt.

CHAPTER NINETEEN

BEZALEL

THE NEXT PERSON TO CONSIDER IS BEZALEL. THOUGH HE'S NOT mentioned in the book of Ezekiel, his vocation and his name have taught me about the watchman lifestyle. Bezalel first appeared in Exodus when God brought him to Moses's attention. "Then the LORD spoke to Moses, saying: 'See, I have called by name Bezalel'" (Exod. 31:1–2). God uniquely gifted Bezalel with His Spirit, with wisdom, and with artistic gifts to construct the Tabernacle and the furniture God showed Moses on the mountain. Bezalel physically built God a house.

What does this "B" man teach us about the vocation of a watchman? His life emphasizes the theme of friendship with God and attentiveness to His presence. Like Bezalel, *the watchmen first and foremost "build" God a house. They must have an insatiable appetite for God's presence and arrange their lives in such a manner that they host Him well.*

Psalm 132:4–5 articulates this aspect of the watchmen sentiment, issuing from David's heart: "I will not give sleep to my eyes or slumber to my eyelids, until I find a place for the LORD, a dwelling place for the Mighty One of Jacob." There is a lot of watchman language in these verses. David's eyes stayed vigilant.

He stayed awake; he stayed focused. Why? He wanted the presence of God. He wanted to be *with Him*. It's the driving motivation of His life. He refused to sleep. He refused to slumber until the LORD had a place in his midst. *Watchmen look for places where God can dwell, where His glory can rest.*

The Eyes of His Glory

Isaiah 3:8 uses an interesting phrase: "the eyes of His glory." What are the "eyes of His glory"? Here is the whole verse: "For Jerusalem stumbled, and Judah is fallen, because their tongue and their doings are against the LORD, to provoke the eyes of His glory." Jerusalem's and Judah's sin provoked "the eyes of His glory." Why? Could it be that these are heavenly eyes, ever roaming the earth, looking for a dwelling place for God's glory? Could it be that David's refusal to let his eyes sleep simply reflected a heavenly reality? Perhaps, heaven has watchmen, and they are always looking for a place that can host the manifested presence of God.

When I look at Scripture with these questions in mind, I find it not only plausible, but also confirmed that heaven has watchmen. Daniel 4 chronicles Nebuchadnezzar's arrogance, humiliation, and restoration. His humiliation began when a watcher from heaven descended to the earth: "I saw in the visions of my head while on my bed, and there was a watcher, a holy one, coming down from heaven" (4:13). The "watcher" pronounced judgment, describing a community of heavenly watchmen that were in agreement with his words: "This decision is by the decree of the watchers, and the sentence by the word of the holy ones." (4:17). When heaven's watchers saw Nebuchadnezzar's arrogance, they agreed he needed to be humbled.

I'm fascinated by the concept that heaven has watchmen. I

wonder if this is who Ezekiel encountered in the whirlwind. Ezekiel 1:5 tells us that it wasn't just a raging fire or the color amber contained within the whirlwind. It also had creatures within it: "Also from within [the whirlwind] came the likeness of four living creatures." Ezekiel went into great detail, describing these odd beings. As I noted earlier, one of their primary features both in Ezekiel and in Revelation is the number of eyes they have: "And their whole body, with their back, and their hands, their wings, and the wheels that the four had, were full of eyes all around" (10:12). Since they are "full of eyes," it's safe to assume they have a watchman role in heaven. This explains further why Ezekiel saw them. He encountered from heaven what he was called to be on the earth.

It's interesting, though, that Ezekiel waited until chapter 10 to mention that their entire bodies are full of eyes. First, he only described their eyes being in one place: "As for their rims, they were so high they were awesome; and their rims were full of eyes." (1:18). Each living creature was accompanied by a wheel that contained within it another wheel. The wheels gave the creatures instant mobility, moving as the Spirit of God directed them. On the rims of these wheels, Ezekiel first saw and described their eyes. Why were eyes specifically on the rims of their wheels?

As the wheels and the creatures moved, they did so in harmony with the glory and throne of God. Twice, Ezekiel described that something like a throne was above their heads:

And *above their firmament over their heads* was the likeness of a throne, in appearance like a sapphire stone; on the likeness of the throne was a likeness with the appearance of a man high above it. (1:26)

And I looked, and there in the firmament that was *above the head of the cherubim,* there appeared something like a sapphire stone, having the appearance of the likeness of a throne. (10:1)

This "likeness of a throne" was not just hovering above their heads, disconnected from the creatures. There was some kind of relationship between the location of the throne and the movement of the creatures. Furthermore, the throne, the creatures, the whirlwind, etc. were all collectively an expression of the glory of God. As the creatures moved out of the Temple in Ezekiel 10, the glory of God departed from the Temple.

> Then the glory of the LORD departed from the threshold of the temple and stood over the cherubim. And the cherubim lifted their wings and mounted from the earth in my sight. When they went out, the wheels were beside them; and they stood at the door of the east gate of the LORD's house, and the glory of the God of Israel was above them. (10:18–19)

Like the Levites bearing the ark of the covenant, these creatures somehow bore the throne of glory, moving as the Spirit moved. What does this teach us about the eyes on the rims of the wheels?

Perhaps, these eyes were specifically what Isaiah referred to when he used the phrase "the eyes of His glory." Since the wheels gave mobility to God's glory, perhaps the eyes on the wheels were looking for a place where His glory could rest. They were looking for a place where they could set the throne, the throne on which sits the burning Man with an amber heart. They were looking for a place that could host Him well. In Ezekiel, when the eyes beheld idolatry in the Temple, they carried away the manifested presence of God. Jerusalem's "tongue and their doings" provoked "the eyes of His glory," so the glory left.

If this is indeed what the heavenly watchmen do, then it is a template for what we are called to do. *We are looking for a dwelling place for God.* Not only are we looking for it, but like Bezalel we are creating it. *We use our time, talents, and treasure to create a landing pad for His throne in our midst. We create atmospheres that accommodate the burning Man with an amber heart.* God wants to give His watchmen "the eyes of His glory." With those eyes, we not only behold His glory ourselves, but also prepare the way for others to see Him.

The Shadow of God

The vocation of this "B" man, Bezalel, gives us a reference point for the watchman vocation. The first thing he teaches us about being a watchman is friendship with God. He built God a house. *Hosting God through intimate companionship is the foundation of the watchman's lifestyle.* However, that's not everything Bezalel teaches us about being a watchman. Not only is his vocation significant, but so is the meaning of his name. Bezalel means "in the shadow of God."[1] *When watchmen build God a house, the result is that cities come under the shadow of God.*

What is the significance of being "in the shadow of God"? Psalm 91 teaches that the shadow of God is the place of God's protection. The imagery is that God hovers above you, guarding you from harm. The psalm is rich in promise after promise, describing God as a shield, deliverer, and refuge. How does someone find themselves in this protected place under God's shadow? The first verse tells us: "He who dwells in the secret place of the Most High shall abide under the shadow of the Almighty." This verse shows us a direct link between Bezalel's vocation and his name. His vocation was to build God a house, so others may "dwell in the secret place of the Most High." The result was that the nation of Israel was able to "abide under the shadow of the Almighty." Like Bezalel, our greatest contribution as watchmen is not just to look to the horizon, but to dwell in the secret place, invoking the shadow of God over our lives.

The call of the watchmen, though, is not only to invoke the shadow of God over their lives individually, but over cities. Imagine what it would look like for Psalm 91 to be expanded beyond one person's home and applied to an entire city. What if it applied to an entire nation? I believe the watchmen have the responsibility to see that happen. As they host God within cities, the shadow of God begins to hover over cities, bringing with it all the benefits of Psalm 91. Bezalel, a man whose name starts with a "B," teaches us that *the secret place of God begets the shadow of God.*

CHAPTER TWENTY

BEZER

THE THIRD "B" NAME TO CONSIDER IS BEZER. IT'S NOT A FAMILIAR name to most of us, and it's not actually the name of a man in Scripture. It's the name of a city. However, many times Scripture personifies cities, referring to them as individuals. Furthermore, Bezer is a city with an intriguing name. It means "an inaccessible spot."[1] Deuteronomy 4:43 describes it as being "in the wilderness on the plateau." Thus, its name is a description of its topography. Bezer was in the wilderness on a plateau in an inaccessible spot. This is a description of its natural features, but I also believe Bezer describes the supernatural features of a city that has watchmen. When watchmen guard a city, it becomes inaccessible to the enemy. Like the promises of Psalm 91, pestilence, arrows, and destruction cannot penetrate a city under the shadow of God.

Levitical Cities

Another intriguing feature of Bezer is that it is a Levitical city. What is a Levitical city? When the children of Israel entered the Promised Land, each tribe had a land inheritance to grow within a certain territory. That is, each tribe had land except the Levites. Instead of inheriting soil, they inherited something far better—the presence of God. Deuteronomy 10:9 explains, "Levi has no portion nor inheritance with his brethren; the LORD is his inheritance." As Israel's consecrated tribe for service in the Tabernacle, their reward was God Himself. However, they had to live somewhere. Thus, when they were not serving in the Tabernacle (and later the Temple), they lived scattered among the other twelve tribes in cities specifically donated to them. Those donated cities were called the Levitical cities, and there was a total of 48 of them. Bezer was one of these special, set apart cities (see Joshua 21:1–42).

What does it mean for a city to be a Levitical city? Levitical cities were consecrated cities because they were inhabited by a consecrated tribe. These cities were not common or ordinary. They were set a part to God for a special use because of the people who dwelt in them.

When watchmen take their place, cities are no longer ordinary, merely existing as places of commerce and residence. *When watchmen take their place, cities become consecrated places that are set apart to the purposes of God.* Cities become places of destiny where God's will is manifested into the earth. This consecration happens not because of the buildings or the streets, but because the people within the city embrace consecration themselves. Remember, it was the consecration of Levites that caused the cities to be consecrated. When the voice of the watchmen is heard and people embrace consecration, then cities begin to take on a different spiritual atmosphere. God-awareness increases, and there is a God-ward movement of hearts.

The greatest way to protect cities from the coming judgment is to call their inhabitants to consecration. The judgment of God is not a randomized lottery. It doesn't fall haphazardly from heaven without rhyme or reason. The garden of Eden shows us the dynamics at play when judgment displaces man from a city. It begins when people incline their ears to the whispers of Satan. That inclination to consider Satan's voice leads to both deception and rebellion. Paul explained that "the woman [was] deceived" (1 Tim. 2:14). Eve acted upon what she thought was right, though it was wrong. Adam, on the other hand, "was not deceived." Instead, he blatantly rebelled against God's commandment, knowing full well what he was doing. *These two results—deception and rebellion—are the consequences of mankind considering Satan's voice.* When we listen to the serpent, we entangle ourselves in confusion regarding the truth, or we grow calloused toward the truth, not caring about what is right or wrong. God will eventually hold us accountable for both conditions. The best way to interrupt this trajectory is for cities, and the inhabitants within cities, to embrace a Levitical, set apart posture toward God. *When you have a mentality of consecration, you don't even consider what the enemy has to say.* Like Jesus, when you recognize Satan is coming, you respond, "He has nothing in Me" (John 14:30).

What made Eve vulnerable to deception? It wasn't that the serpent mounted a convincing argument. After Satan spoke, the Bible didn't say, "When the serpent made sense to the woman, she took the fruit." There were other factors at play. It says, "So when the woman saw that the tree was good for food, that it was pleasant to the eyes, and a tree desirable to make one wise, she took of its fruit and ate" (Gen. 3:6). This verse lists three things that pulled Eve into deception: (1) she "saw that the tree was good for food," (2) she saw "it was pleasant to the eyes," and (3) she saw that it was "a tree desirable to make one wise." Each of these are appetite-based things. They are not reason-based things. They appeal to humanity's appetite for the world—for pleasure outside of God and His commandments. In 1 John 2:16, the apostle wrote about these three factors, giving them New Testament language. It says, "For all that is in the world—the lust of the flesh, the lust of the eyes, and the pride of life—is not of the Father but is of the world." The "lust of the flesh" corresponds to Eve seeing "the tree was good for food." It tasted good to her senses, though God forbade it. The "lust of the eyes" corresponds to seeing the tree as "pleasant to the eyes." It was alluring, tempting to the gaze. The "pride of life" corresponds to the tree being "desirable to make one wise." Not only did it taste good and look good, but it made us look good in the estimation of other people. Again, these are things of the appetite and not logic. Thus, the answer to overcoming them is not a better argument against Satan's reasoning. The answer is having a consecrated heart that has a sanctified appetite for God.

Man's appetite for sin leads him into deception. If man submits his appetite to God, it closes the door to deception. Consecration is a key to protecting cities. Again, the judgment of God does not descend randomly. The deception of Satan partners with the rebellion of man, eventually leading to the judgment of God. However, the intercession and preaching of the watchmen can interrupt that trajectory.

Cities of Refuge

The third intriguing element of Bezer is that it was also a city of refuge. Throughout Israel, 6 of the 48 Levitical cities were also appointed to be cities of refuge. These cities offered protection to anyone who had killed a neighbor unintentionally. The manslayer could stay there until the avenger had died (see Num. 35 and Josh. 21). Consequently, the city became a safe place for those who needed protection. *When watchmen guard cities, the cities become harbors for people who need a safe place to go.* Imagine what it would look like if your city became well known for God-happenings? Imagine what it would look like if people heard the name of your city and immediately thought about a move of God? Your city would become a city of refuge, a safe place for people to come and/or bring those who need God-encounters.

It's not mere fantastical thinking to imagine cities as Levitical centers. Psalm 125:3 gives this promise: "For the scepter of wickedness shall not rest on the land allotted to the righteous."

When God has given a city into the hands of the righteous, evil's authority ("the scepter of wickedness") cannot "rest" or stay. *The intercession of the righteous shatters the prevailing spiritual atmosphere that influences people toward disobedience. That doesn't remove people's free will within the city, but it does shift the current of the spirit.* The rest of the verse explains, "Lest the righteous reach out their hands to iniquity." When "the scepter of wickedness" rests on a city, even the righteous have a propensity toward iniquity. When that authority is broken, not only do the righteous continue to live righteously, but the unrighteous experience God-cravings.

During the First Great Awakening, Jonathan Edwards wrote about this shift in his journals. He gave a first-hand account of the transformation of his town, Northampton, Massachusetts, writing, "[A] great and earnest concern about the great things of religion and the eternal world became universal in all parts of the town and among persons of all degrees and all ages. The noise of the dry bones waxes louder and louder."[2] As the sound of revival increased, everyone came under the sway of the Spirit, even those who were typically "vainest and loosest" and those who "were not generally subject to great awakenings."[3] Edwards went on to write about the way the very atmosphere of his city changed:

> This work of God, as it was carried on and the number of true saints multiplied, soon made a glorious alteration in the town, so that in the spring and summer following, Anno 1735, the town seemed to be full of the presence of God. It never was so full of love, nor so full of joy . . . there were remarkable tokens of God's presence in almost every house.[4]

This entry is stunning to me, and it stirs my appetite for revival. If God could break into a city during the 1730s, He can do it again, today. Surely, if we take our place as watchmen, then we can see what Jonathan Edwards saw when he wrote, "And the work of conversion was carried on in a most astonishing manner and increased more and more; souls did, as it were, come by flocks to Jesus Christ."[5] *Your intercession gathers souls, and it changes cities.*

Edwards also recorded how Northampton became a "city of refuge" for others. He said, "There were many instances of persons that came from abroad, on visits or business . . . [who] partook of that shower of divine blessing that God rained down here . . . ."[6] As travelers came to his city, they found God. And the God-encounter didn't stay with them only as long as they were in Northampton. What people encountered there spread with them to other cities:

> [At] length the same work began to appear and prevail in several other towns in the country. In the month of March, the people in South Hadley began to be seized with a deep concern about the things of religion, which very soon became universal. . . . About the same time, it began to break forth in the west part of Suffield . . . and it soon spread into all parts of the town. It next appear at Sunderland. . . . In every place, God brought His saving blessings with Him, and His Word, attended with His Spirit . . . returned not void.[7]

Northampton served as a city of refuge for people to find God. Then, that set off a chain reaction that spread like wildfire. City after city became consecrated places. Their inhabitants received the gospel and surrendered their lives to God.

Not only do these kinds of shifts bring individuals into God's Kingdom, but also they fortify cities, preserving them for the purposes of God. As I wrote earlier, the best way to protect cities is to call the inhabitants of cities into consecration. Psalm 12:8 says, "The wicked prowl on every side, when vileness is exalted among the sons of men." When "vileness" becomes a pursuit, an exalted goal, then danger surrounds the destiny of a city. Conversely, righteousness serves as a breastplate, establishing and guarding the gates.

Bezer highlights the intercessory, city-vocation of the watchmen. Remember the dream: "God is looking for watchmen, or cities will be no more." Without watchmen, cities are vulnerable to Satan's schemes and set themselves against God, provoking judgment. With watchmen, the trajectory of cities change. The protective shadow of God hovers above them. They are inaccessible to the enemy. *Like the angel guarding the tree of life, watchmen guard the gates of cities.* Their intercessory work is not just protective, though. It is proactive. It brings cities *into* destiny as consecrated places. It brings them into their identity as cities of refuge where others can find God and find rest for their souls. Let Bezer stoke your imagination for what it could look like if the shadow of God rested upon your city.

CHAPTER TWENTY-ONE

BARUCH

The last "B" man we'll consider is Baruch. The book of Jeremiah describes his vocation, and from that we will glean insights about the watchman lifestyle. In Jeremiah 36, God told Jeremiah, "Take a scroll of a book and write on it all the words that I have spoken to you against Israel, against Judah, and against all the nations, from the day I have spoken to you." (v. 2). Jeremiah obeyed God by employing a scribe named "Baruch." Baruch's vocation was to write down everything God said. Not only did he write it, but he also read it to everyone in the Temple on Jeremiah's behalf. Through writing, he recorded what God said, and through preaching, he bore witness to what God said

First, it is essential for watchmen to record what God says. We need to know the Lord's counsel. We've covered this already throughout the book, but it bears repeating that we cannot interact with the world around us based upon our own opinions. It's not our brilliance or our innovative speech that turns the human heart to God. It is the word of the Lord. We need to know *and remember* His counsel. It is one thing to know it. It is another thing to *remember* it. Many times, Israel floundered because she forgot the Lord and His commandments. *Watchmen look for the Lord's present counsel. They also remember the Lord's former counsel.*

They serve as both the eyes of the nation *and* the memory of the nation. Their record of prophetic history presents both warnings and promises. They use both as fuel for intercession.

In his message, "How I Became Involved with Israel," Derek Prince described how one of the Hebrew words for "watchman" is related to "secretary." He then explained that one of a secretary's responsibilities is to remind the boss of his or her appointments. *The secretary is familiar with previous commitments, and he or she recalls them to mind. In the same way, watchmen remind God of His previous commitments. Watchmen are familiar with the promises God has made, and they use them in intercession, imploring God to act accordingly.*

Scripture is filled with examples of people who not only reminded God of His promises, but they agitated God with their prayers. In Isaiah 62 (the most well-known watchman chapter), it gives an explicit charge for the watchmen to do this, saying, "I have set watchmen on your walls, O Jerusalem; they shall never hold their peace day or night. You who make mention of the LORD, do not keep silent, and *give Him no rest* till He establishes and till He makes Jerusalem a praise in the earth" (vv. 6–7). These verses tell the watchmen to "give Him no rest." Give who no rest? Give God no rest. Isaiah gave the watchmen a job description, and it included keeping God awake. Agitating Him. Reminding Him over and over of what He promised to do, and staying continually in this mode of aggravation until God did what He said.

Jesus Himself affirmed that this posture of prayer is not only permissible, but fruitful. In Luke 11, the disciples asked Jesus to teach them to pray. After giving them the model prayer, He then immediately gave them a parable to teach them the right *posture* of prayer. He told them a story of someone who annoyed his friend at midnight, asking over and over for bread. Eventually, the friend in bed got up and gave the man bread. Jesus explained, "I say to you, though he will not rise and give to him because he is his friend, yet because of his persistence he will rise and give him as many as he needs" (11:8). *According to Jesus, the right way to pray is persistence that annoys God.* Though He seems reluctant, He actually likes the agitation, and He responds with plenty.

This isn't an isolated story, either. Later in Luke 18:1–8, Jesus taught another parable on prayer. Like the friend at midnight, it affirms the aggressive posture of annoying God. A widow demanded justice from a judge. The judge, however, was "unjust." He didn't "fear God nor regard man." Eventually, though, the judge granted her request. Why? Jesus explained, "And he would not [answer her] for a while; but afterward he said within himself, 'Though I do not fear God nor regard man, yet because this widow troubles me I will avenge her, lest by her continual coming she weary me.'" She prevailed because, like the watchmen in Isaiah 62, she gave him "no rest." Like the friend at midnight, her "persistence" provoked an answer. This is how Jesus taught us to pray! Though our God doesn't slumber, and though our God is not unjust, we still ought to approach Him as if we are trying to wake Him and trying to provoke Him to action. Though our God doesn't forget, we still remind Him of what He said until we see what He said in full reality around us.

Baruch teaches us to record and remember what God speaks. We do this in order to pray it to God *and* speak it to others. *Knowing what God says gives us a voice in the heavens and a voice on the earth.* Though we may think of the prophets as innovative poets, a closer look reveals something different. They did not invent or originate what they prophesied. Their prophetic utterances were poetic renderings of what God previously had said to their forefathers, such as Abraham, Moses, and David. The judgments they prophesied restated the curses of the Law. The promises they released reaffirmed in elaborate ways God's blessings on obedience, repentance, and returning to Him. The Spirit took old truth, baptized it with fresh revelation within the heart of the prophets, and released through them a timely message for their audience. Because the prophets knew what God *said,* they were able to release what God was saying.

In his essay "Traditional and the Individual Talent," T. S. Eliot described the vanity of poets who aspire to pure innovation. Instead, they must add their individual talent to the tradition of truth as it has been revealed through the development of literary works. To do this, they must fully digest what has been written before. They can't have a knowledge of literature that is narrow in scope or immature in its understanding. Rather, they must saturate their minds in truth and write with intentional literary consciousness. Eliot modeled this himself, filling his poetry with layers of allusions that were explicit, subtle, and beautifully executed. Eliot's mind and manner demonstrate something of the watchman. *For our voices to find their full range of impact, our eyes, ears, and minds must be saturated, fixated, and keen to remember the truth God has revealed in the past.* Eliot wrote that the poet cannot "take the past as a lump, an indiscriminate bolus." A "bolus" is "a small, rounded lump of a substance, especially partly digested food."[1] What Eliot was saying was that merely consuming literature without fully digesting it will only produce something trite. The poet must instead absorb literature's tensions, nuances, beauty, and tragedy. In the same way, the watchmen need to be intimately acquainted with what God has said. They ought to set aside time to ponder and pray. They must eat the scroll until it becomes a part of them.

The House of Israel

There is one last thing Baruch teaches us about the watchmen that we need to cover before this book concludes. In fact, to ignore it would be to leave the watchmen teaching incomplete. That topic is Israel. I will only introduce it here because to thoroughly cover it would require another book. While the watchmen theme is applicable for every nation and every city on earth, it also has a specific and unique application for one city and one nation on earth. That nation is Israel, and that city is Jerusalem. *Baruch called the watchmen to be witnesses to Israel of God's promises and to prepare her for the Lord's return.*

In Jeremiah 36, Baruch played the general role of writing down everything God spoke to Jeremiah. In Jeremiah 32, he played a much more specific role. In that chapter, God told Jeremiah to buy a field. It was a sign of God's promises to Israel, denoting the recovery of lost land and the redemption of a lost people. Once Jeremiah purchased the field, he then gave a weighty responsibility to Baruch:

> I gave the purchase deed to Baruch. . . . Then I charged Baruch before them, saying, "Thus says the LORD of hosts, the God of Israel: 'Take these deeds, both this purchase deed which is sealed and this deed which is open, and put them in an earthen vessel, that they may last many days.'" (32:12–14)

Baruch became the caretaker of the purchase deeds. He had to protect them "that they may last many days." In doing this, Baruch was not just caring for documents. He was protecting what the deeds represent: the promises of God. He became their keeper in order to be a living witness to Israel in the days when it seemed all hope was lost.

As watchmen, we must keep God's promises to Israel close to our hearts, within our own personal "earthen vessel." Israel has faced, does face, and will face days of trouble. *As she does, it is the watchmen's responsibility to do what Baruch did: record and remember. We must remind her of God's faithfulness. And we must agitate God until He acts faithfully.*

Baruch's vocation calls us to an Israel-specific role as watchmen. Interestingly, his name does as well. It means "blessed."[2] It comes from the word in Hebrew that opens Psalm 118:26, saying *"Blessed* is he who comes in the name of the LORD." This verse has a direct connection to Jerusalem's future. When Jesus wept for the city of Jerusalem, He quoted Psalm 118:26: "I say to you [Jerusalem], you shall see Me no more till you say, 'Blessed is He who comes in the name of the LORD'" (Matt. 23:39). Jesus is waiting for the day when Jerusalem is ready to receive Him as King. He is waiting on her to say, "Baruch," to Him. *As Baruch-watchmen, we have a role to play in that process. Our witness and our intercession open the ancient gates of Jerusalem by calling her heart to Jesus the King.*

Remember, to be a watchman is to watch *with Him*. It is to lean into friendship with God. He is not just a watchman generally. He is a watchman specifically for Israel. As Psalm 121:4 says, "Behold, He who keeps [*šāmar*] Israel shall neither slumber nor sleep." If we want to be with Him as He watches, then in some measure our prophetic sensitivity, intercessory heart, and missional obedience will connect to Jerusalem. From the whirlwind of God's amber heart, may we, like Ezekiel, hear these words: "Son of man, I have made you a watchman *for the house of Israel*" (Ezek. 3:17).

PART SIX
CONCLUSION

CHAPTER TWENTY-TWO

INSTRUCTION AND IMPARTATION

I want to end this book by describing two aspects of God's Word. It's my prayer this book has contained both.

Sometimes, when God speaks, it is *instruction*. He informs us of something He wants us to learn, embrace, adopt, and implement into our lives. At other times, when He speaks, it is *impartation*. In that scenario, He's not just telling us something to learn or do. He is literally giving us something at the very moment He says it. Our role is then to simply activate what we have received from Him and then guard its operation in our lives.

In Acts 10, we find an example of a visionary encounter that is instruction from God. As Peter prayed, he saw all kinds of unclean animals that God commanded him to eat. When Peter objected, God responded, "What God has cleansed you must not call common" (Acts 10:15). As Peter pondered the vision, men from Cornelius's house inquired after him. Eventually, he found himself preaching the gospel for the first time to Gentiles. The vision became a clear reference point for Peter. As God cleansed the Gentiles through the gospel, Peter must not call them common or unclean. He must embrace them into the household of faith. The vision was instruction.

Another example is in Acts 26. Paul recounted his conversion experience, which included a call to preach the gospel. Paul then said, "Therefore, King Agrippa, I was not disobedient to the heavenly vision, but declared first to those in Damascus and in Jerusalem, and throughout all the region of Judea, and then to the Gentiles, that they should repent, turn to God, and do works befitting repentance" (Acts 26:19–20). The "heavenly vision" was instruction for Paul to obey. He spent his life responding to what God told Him to do.

An example of impartation is in 1 Kings 3 when Solomon asked God for "an understanding heart." I put this into the category of an encounter because the event happened within a dream. Thus, it wasn't fully certain that Solomon was an active participant in what he was doing. Because it was within a dream, he was more of a recipient. What really intrigues me is that, when Solomon woke up, he didn't do what the dream said. Let me explain: If I had had Solomon's dream in 1 Kings 3, I would have woken up, written it down, and then treated it as instruction. I would have asked the Lord for an understanding heart, assuming that was what God was telling me to do. Instead, Solomon didn't ask for it. Upon waking up, he offered sacrifices to God in gratitude, acting as though he had already received it: "Then Solomon awoke; and indeed it had been a dream. And he came to Jerusalem and stood before the ark of the covenant of the LORD, offered up burnt offerings, offered peace offerings, and made a feast for all his servants" (1 Kings 3:15). The dream was not telling Solomon what to do. The dream was revealing to Solomon what God was doing. This is confirmed in the very next passage of Scripture. It's the famous story of two women arguing over a baby. After Solomon justly resolved the situation, this was the result: "And all Israel heard of the judgment which the king had rendered; and they feared the king, for they saw that the wisdom of God was in him to administer justice" (3:28). The dream imparted to him the "wisdom of God." God's word to him was an impartation *of* something, not just instruction *for* something.

When Solomon awoke, he already had what God had spoken about.

The next example of an impartation is one that very much concerns us. It's Ezekiel and the whirlwind. When God dropped him from the whirlwind, He didn't say, "Ezekiel, learn to be a watchman." Instead, God spoke about what He Himself had done: "Son of man, I have made you a watchman" (Ezek. 3:17). This work of God is repeated throughout the book. In Ezekiel 12:6, God said to him, "I have made you a sign to the house of Israel." Later, God repeated the original watchman statement, saying, "So you, son of man: I have made you a watchman for the house of Israel" (Ezek. 33:7). The watchman call was not just something God *instructed*. It was something God *imparted*. God made Ezekiel into something he had not been before. Ezekiel still had responsibility to embrace the commission, but it was God who sovereignly gave him the gifts needed to do that.

Impartation establishes you in the calling God gives you. In Romans 1:11, Paul wrote, "I long to see you, that I may impart to you some spiritual gift, so that you may be established." Paul envisioned and anticipated ministering among the Romans—not just to teach them or pastor them, but to *impart* spiritual gifts to them. As a result, the Romans would be "established" in a greater way. If you only learn about something in God's Kingdom without *receiving* something from God about that topic, then your application will waver in its force and consistency. The Kingdom of God is receptivity based rather than being a mental ascent. Hebrews 12:28 says, "Therefore, since we are *receiving* a kingdom which cannot be shaken. . . ." We receive the Kingdom, and then it renews our minds according to its realities. Receiving an impartation establishes you into a calling in a transformational way.

God is able to impart the watchman call to us because, as I described in chapter 4, He Himself is the ultimate Watchman. An impartation from God's Spirit is not simply a gift from Him, but it's an infusion of Him into our souls. When you look at Jesus, you see the kind of watchman God is making you.

We could walk through Jesus's life and identify the characteristics of holy interruption, friendship with God, prophetic sensitivity, intercessory love, and missional obedience. However, let's focus on only one insightful moment. The first Palm Sunday gives us a glimpse into Jesus the Watchman.

We typically think of Palm Sunday as a day of triumph. Jesus seemed to victoriously ride into Jerusalem, heralded as King, fulfilling prophecy and bringing salvation. However, if you could have looked closer at Jesus's face on that day, you would have seen the glimmer of tears.

Before Jesus ascended to Jerusalem on the donkey, He first descended from the Mount of Olives, crossing the Kidron Valley. While He rode, tears descended from His eyes. Luke recorded, "Now as He drew near, He saw the city and wept over it" (19:41). Though crowds lauded Him with praise, His heart ached. Why? The city Jesus loved was not prepared to receive Him as King. Exuberant crowds may have surrounded Jesus, but those crowds came primarily from Bethany—not Jerusalem (see John 12:17). In fact, when He entered Jerusalem, the inhabitants of the city asked, "Who is this?" (Matt. 21:10). They did not recognize their King.

Those tears revealed the compassionate heart of Jesus concerning Jerusalem. He was not indifferent to its rejection of Him. Unlike Jonah toward Nineveh, Jesus did not relish the possibility of coming judgment. When He saw it, He wept, like Abraham for Sodom. When Jesus knew that her house would be left desolate, He cried out, "O Jerusalem, Jerusalem!" (Matt. 23:37–38).

The tears of Jesus have the power to create change. When He wept for Lazarus, Lazarus didn't stay in the grave. Lazarus went through death, but He didn't end there. Jesus raised Lazarus from the dead. In the same way, because Jesus wept for Jerusalem, her story isn't over. In AD 70, Jerusalem faced destruction at the hands of the Romans, but today she is a thriving city with God-purposes in her future. Jerusalem was in danger of becoming no more, but God found a Watchman—His Son, Jesus. In the

Gospels, Jerusalem rejected Jesus, but He prophesied she would say to Him in the future, "Blessed is He who comes in the name of the LORD!" (Matt. 23:39). The full impact of His tears for Jerusalem are yet to be seen.

God wants to give you this kind of covenantal love, prophetic authority, and potency in prayer for your city, too. My prayer is that through this book you have received not only instruction, but also impartation. Though I hope you have learned, my greatest desire is that you have received. My prayer is that the Spirit of God has interrupted you with God's burning heart, bringing you into deeper places of friendship, prophetic sensitivity, intercessory love, and missional obedience. I pray you have a fresh grace to stay awake, stay focused, and stay pure, embracing the rhythms of the watchman lifestyle.

As the instruction and impartation of this message alter your life, remember that the inconvenience has a purpose. The whirlwind from God has an amber heart burning at the center. That heart beats for souls, for the wellbeing of humanity. As God told Ezekiel, He takes "no pleasure in the death of the wicked, but that the wicked turn from his way and live." God asked Jonah, "Should I not pity Nineveh, that great city, in which are more than 120,000 persons . . . ?" God is not indifferent to the condition of cities, and He is looking for watchmen to partner with Him through their tears. Like Jeremiah, may our lamentations resound in the corridors of heaven and throughout the streets of cities. Like Micah, may we "wail like jackals" until God answers us. May we join the Isaiah 62 watchmen on the walls of Jerusalem who give God no rest day or night. May the tears of Jesus Himself find their way through our eyes.

The Day of the Lord is coming, and cities may be no more. Therefore, God is looking for watchmen who will prepare the way. May He find you and make you into the watchman He needs in this hour for the cities of the earth. May the amber heart of God disrupt your world.

NOTES

1. CAUGHT IN THE WHIRLWIND

1. Wikipedia contributors, "COVID-19 lockdowns," *Wikipedia, The Free Encyclopedia,* accessed July 1, 2024, https://en.wikipedia.org/w/index.php?title=COVID-19_lockdowns&oldid=1230934085.
2. James Glentworth Butler. *Bible-Work: The Old Testament: Vol. 9: Ezekiel–Malachi.* (The Butler Bible-Work Company, 1894), 469.
3. "Land of Israel: Geographical Survey." *Encyclopedia.* October 14, 2024, https://www.encyclopedia.com/religion/encyclopedias-almanacs-transcripts-and-maps/land-israel-geographical-survey.
4. Henry H. Halley, *Halley's Bible Handbook: An Abbreviated Bible Commentary* (Zondervan Publishing House, 1965), 366.

2. CITIES WILL BE NO MORE

1. A. W. Tozer, *The Knowledge of the Holy: The Attributes of God: Their Meaning in the Christian Life* (HarperSanFrancisco, 1961), 36.
2. Tozer, *Knowledge of the Holy,* 89.

4. FRIENDSHIP WITH GOD

1. Live event, December 2004.
2. "H8104 - šāmar - Strong's Hebrew Lexicon (nkjv)," *Blue Letter Bible,* accessed November 2, 2024, https://www.blueletterbible.org/lexicon/h8104/nkjv/wlc/0-1/.

7. INTERCESSORY LOVE

1. J. R. R. Tolkien, *The Two Towers: Being the Second Part of the Lord of the Rings* (William Morrow, 1954), 656.

8. MISSIONAL OBEDIENCE

1. A. W. Tozer, *The Knowledge of the Holy: The Attributes of God: Their Meaning in the Christian Life* (HarperSanFrancisco, 1961), 84.
2. "G5257 - hypēretēs - Strong's Greek Lexicon (nkjv)," *Blue Letter Bible.* accessed November 2, 2024, https://www.blueletterbible.org/lexicon/g5257/nkjv/tr/0-1/.

9. THE COUNSEL OF THE LORD

1. "H1875 - dāraš - Strong's Hebrew Lexicon (nkjv)," *Blue Letter Bible*, accessed November 2, 2024, https://www.blueletterbible.org/lexicon/h1875/nkjv/wlc/0-1/.

2. "H3041 - yᵊdîdyâ - Strong's Hebrew Lexicon (kjv)," *Blue Letter Bible*, accessed November 1, 2024, https://www.blueletterbible.org/lexicon/h3041/kjv/wlc/0-1/.

3. "H8085 - šāmaʿ - Strong's Hebrew Lexicon (kjv)," *Blue Letter Bible*, accessed November 1, 2024, https://www.blueletterbible.org/lexicon/h8085/kjv/wlc/0-1/.

10. THE CONDITION OF YOUR SOUL

1. Edward Bickersteth, *A Treatise on Prayer: Deigned to Assist in Its Devout Discharge* (London, 1819) 68.

2. "H5341 - nāṣar - Strong's Hebrew Lexicon (kjv)," *Blue Letter Bible*, accessed November 1, 2024, https://www.blueletterbible.org/lexicon/h5341/kjv/wlc/0-1/.

11. THE CONDITION OF OUR COMMUNITY

1. Oswald Chambers, *My Utmost for His Highest: Classic Language* (Baker Publishing Group), 248, Kindle.

2. Chambers, *My Utmost*, 182.

13. THE ANSWERS TO OUR PRAYERS

1. Bill Johnson, *Open Heavens: Position Yourself to Encounter the God of Revival* (Destiny Image, Inc.), 55–56, Kindle.

14. THE RETURN OF THE LORD

1. "G2015 - epiphaneia - Strong's Greek Lexicon (kjv)," *Blue Letter Bible*, accessed November 1, 2024, https://www.blueletterbible.org/lexicon/g2015/kjv/tr/0-1/.

15. STAY AWAKE

1. "SURFEIT definition and meaning | Collins English Dictionary," *Collins English Dictionary*, accessed November 1, 2024, https://www.collinsdictionary.com/dictionary/english/surfeit.

16. STAY FOCUSED

1. A. W. Tozer, *The Knowledge of the Holy: The Attributes of God: Their Meaning in the Christian Life* (HarperSanFrancisco, 1961), 116.
2. Tozer, *Knowledge of the Holy*, 116.
3. Tozer, *Knowledge of the Holy*, 71.
4. Tozer, *Knowledge of the Holy*, vii.
5. Tozer, *Knowledge of the Holy*, 43.

17. STAY PURE

1. James Luce, *Chasing Davis: An Atheist's Guide to Morality Using Logic and Science* (iUniverse, Inc., 2012), 359.

18. BUZI

1. "H941 - bûzî - Strong's Hebrew Lexicon (kjv)," *Blue Letter Bible*, accessed November 1, 2024, https://www.blueletterbible.org/lexicon/h941/kjv/wlc/0-1/.
2. "H7043 - qālal - Strong's Hebrew Lexicon (kjv)," *Blue Letter Bible*, accessed November 1, 2024, https://www.blueletterbible.org/lexicon/h7043/kjv/wlc/0-1/.
3. Mark S. Kinzer, *Jerusalem Crucified, Jerusalem Risen: The Resurrected Messiah, the Jewish People, and the Land of Promise* (Cascade Books, 2018), 70.

19. BEZALEL

1. "H1212 - bᵊṣal'ēl - Strong's Hebrew Lexicon (nkjv)," *Blue Letter Bible*, accessed November 2, 2024, https://www.blueletterbible.org/lexicon/h1212/nkjv/wlc/0-1/.

20. BEZER

1. "H1221 - beṣer - Strong's Hebrew Lexicon (nkjv)," *Blue Letter Bible*, accessed November 2, 2024, https://www.blueletterbible.org/lexicon/h1221/nkjv/wlc/0-1/.
2. Peter Marshall and David Manuel. *The Light and the Glory* (Fleming H. Revell, 1977), 296.
3. Marshall and Manuel, *Light and the Glory*, 296.
4. Marshall and Manuel, *Light and the Glory*, 296.
5. Marshall and Manuel, *Light and the Glory*, 296.
6. Marshall and Manuel, *Light and the Glory*, 296.
7. Marshall and Manuel, *Light and the Glory*, 296.

21. BARUCH

1. "BOLUS | English meaning - Cambridge Dictionary," *Cambridge Dictionary*, accessed November 1, 2004, https://dictionary.cambridge.org/dictionary/english/bolus.
2. "H1263 - bārûḵ - Strong's Hebrew Lexicon (nkjv)," *Blue Letter Bible*, accessed November 2, 2024, https://www.blueletterbible.org/lexicon/h1263/nkjv/wlc/0-1/.

ABOUT THE AUTHOR

For over 20 years, Micah Wood has served in leadership at the Ramp, a global youth and young adult ministry based in Hamilton, Alabama. His roles have included Director of Ramp University, Lead Pastor of Ramp Church with his wife, Delana, and International Advancement Pastor, which took his family to Manchester, United Kingdom. Micah recently joined the ministry Eagles' Wings, headquartered in Buffalo, New York. He oversees the Eagles' Wings pastors network, the Israel Christian Nexus, which builds bridges between the Jewish and Christian communities through education, relationship, and advocacy.

In 2012, Micah co-authored *Simple Devotion*, teaching how to answer the call to discipleship through a lifestyle of prayer.

Micah and Delana currently live in Manchester with their four children. Learn more at www.micahwood.org.

Printed in Great Britain
by Amazon

57552639R00121